Happiness is a Rare Bird

To Brian

Gene Walz

Pileated Woodpecker

Happiness is a Rare Bird
Living the Birding Life

by
Gene Walz

TURNSTONE PRESS

Happiness is a Rare Bird: Living the Birding Life
copyright © Gene Walz 2016

Turnstone Press
Artspace Building
206-100 Arthur Street
Winnipeg, MB
R3B 1H3 Canada
www.TurnstonePress.com

All rights reserved. No part of this book may be reproduced or transmitted in any form or by any means—graphic, electronic or mechanical—without the prior written permission of the publisher. Any request to photocopy any part of this book shall be directed in writing to Access Copyright, Toronto.

Turnstone Press gratefully acknowledges the assistance of the Canada Council for the Arts, the Manitoba Arts Council, the Government of Canada through the Canada Book Fund, and the Province of Manitoba through the Book Publishing Tax Credit and the Book Publisher Marketing Assistance Program.

Printed and bound in Canada by Friesens for Turnstone Press.

Pileated Woodpecker image on page ii by Kathryn Manix Walz.

Library and Archives Canada Cataloguing in Publication

Walz, Eugene P., author
    Happiness is a rare bird : living the birding life / by Gene Walz.

Issued in print and electronic formats.

ISBN 978-0-88801-583-9 (softcover).--ISBN 978-0-88801-585-3 (Kindle).
--ISBN 978-0-88801-584-6 (EPUB).--ISBN 978-0-88801-586-0 (PDF)

    1. Walz, Eugene P. 2. Bird watchers--Canada--Biography.
3. Bird watching. I. Title.

QL31.W26A3 2016   598.092   C2016-907578-8
                                        C2016-907579-6

*To my grandsons Torsten and Theo
I don't need bluebirds; my happiness is you.*

*To Buddy, long-time furry companion
His daily dog walks allowed me to conceive
and mull over many of these ideas.*

Contents

Preface / ix

Even Common Birds Can Be Special
House Sparrows: Basic, Economy-sized Birds / 5
Black-capped Chickadees: Cheerful, Little Fluffballs / 8
Mallards and Other Tippy Ducks / 11
Nuthatches and Woodpeckers: Birds with Sticky Feet / 14
A Great Blue Heron Returns Before Ice-out / 17
American White Pelicans: Ghost Riders in the Sky / 19
Eyeball to Eyeball with a Short-eared Owl / 21
Merlins and Other Bird Brains / 24
Corvids: The Smartest Birds in the World / 27
Kathy and the Pileated Woodpeckers / 31

What Is So Rare As
Atlantic Puffins: Clowns of the Sea / 37
A Gray-crowned Rosy-Finch: Truculent Vagabond / 40
Mississippi Kites: Alien Visitors / 43
Northern Cardinal: Rare Bird, Alert / 47
Indigo Bunting or Lazuli: What the Heck Is It? / 50
A Greylag and Other Wild Goose Chases / 53
Burrowing Owls: A Trip to FortWhyte Alive / 56
Apapanes and Other Hawaiian Birds / 60
Andean Cock of the Rock: The Bird Gods Smile on Us / 62
Antpittas: The Bird Gods Spurn Us / 65
Forty-spotted Pardalotes: Rare Australian Endemic / 68
The Resplendent Quetzal: My Favourite Bird / 72
Hummingbirds: A Divine Pash / 75

Once in a Lifetime Birding Experiences
Broad-winged Hawks: An Unexpected Spectacle / 83
Fast and Furious Falcons / 89
A Fall-out of Spring Warblers / 92
Eight Things I've Seen with My Own Two Eyes / 95
Bob Nero and the Great Grey Owl / 108
Churchill, Manitoba: A Birder's Chilly Paradise / 111
The Big Spit: At a Birding Festival / 115
Vietnam North to South / 123
My Birding Bruises / 136
Looking for Potoos: A Deadly Encounter / 139
Scary Surprise on an Amazonian Birding Tower / 141
Big Jags and Bad Drivers / 144
Terrible Trees and Few Birds: A Christmas Story / 148

Things That Don't Make Me Happy, People Who Do
Common Grackles: Unloved and Unwanted / 155
Wrynecks and Other Jinx Birds / 158
What's in a Name? / 161
The Passenger Pigeon Apocalypse / 164
Bird Feeder Freeloaders / 168
Bird-Guiding: Not as Tempting as It Seems / 170
Nerdy? No Way! / 173
The Old Man and the Lek / 176
Old Jack and the Crow with One Leg / 179
Bob Taylor: The Funniest Birder Ever / 181
Wooly Bears, Not Birds / 185

Preface

For me, nothing can quite match the pleasure and satisfaction of finding a rare bird.

Whether that bird is in a foreign land, or in a place it isn't supposed to be, or it just doesn't get seen very often because its numbers have been greatly reduced, the feeling can be overwhelming. It's the birding equivalent of finding a truly exceptional relic—a dinosaur bone, an ancient gold coin, or a painting bought for two dollars and valued at twenty thousand. It's worth the *Antiques Roadshow*'s most frequent response: "Wow!" It's a delightful moment, a thrilling moment.

You feel like the planets have somehow aligned in your favor, the birding gods have bestowed an unexpected gift on you—a fabulous bird, like something out of a fable.

Finding a rare bird is exceptionally satisfying if you're with other savvy birders, even if they've already seen your "lifer"—a bird you're seeing for the first time. Handshakes or high-fives are exchanged. A celebratory beverage often follows. All's right with the world.

That's what happened when a Rustic Bunting showed up in Creighton, Saskatchewan several years ago. Creighton is just across the border from Flin Flon, Manitoba, one of the most amusingly named towns in North America. (Look it up!) It's about 800 kilometres (500 miles) from my home in Winnipeg, one way. 1,000 miles round trip. It was mid-winter. The roads were icy. Yet carloads of birders made the nine-hour—one way—drive on the off-chance that they would catch a glimpse of a small, non-descript bird. I was in one of those cars. We all admitted we were more than a little nuts.

Gene Walz

The Rustic Bunting shouldn't be anywhere near Saskatchewan. It's a Eurasian species that is an uncommon migrant to the Aleutian Islands in spring and rare there in the fall. Sometimes it's an accidental visitor along the coastline of British Columbia. Its inland appearance, in northern Saskatchewan of all places, was a significant birding event.

We started off in the utter darkness at 5:00 am. We couldn't see anything, but then again, going through the barren Interlake and the boreal forest, there wasn't much to see at the best of times. In nervous anticipation, we shared stories in the darkened car of the rare birds that we were lucky enough to have seen. Then we switched to the whiffs—the trips we'd made in search of a rarity when we'd come up empty. I once made four trips to Portage la Prairie trying to spot a Scissor-tailed Flycatcher, an elegant grey and white bird with salmon-coloured flanks and an absurdly long, forked tail; it had somehow wandered from its normal range in Texas and Oklahoma. To find that flycatcher, I travelled 150 miles each trip. No luck. Emotional mayhem: self-doubt, frustration, rising amounts of anger and disappointment.

With the bunting, things were different. We got to Creighton and spotted the bunting almost immediately. Whew! Relief and elation. Our long trip was not in vain. The little bird was coming to a feeder with a handful of sparrows and Juncos. The couple that owned the house and supplied seeds for the feeder invited us inside to warm up; they poured us celebrity cups of tea (not our usual lifer libation). We stayed for maybe twenty minutes and then hopped in the car and drove all the way back to Winnipeg. Crazy! My daughters had a term for us: "Daffy Birdwatchers."

What made the trip even more memorable, however, was not just the bunting or the tea-time hospitality of the feeder owners. On our trip we all got our first close-up view of a herd of woodland caribou, the so-called ghosts of the forest. They were shorter than any of us had imagined. We also saw a lynx, bigger than we thought and capable of leaping more than its height to pounce on something (a vole?) under the snow. And we were able to count a goshawk, not exactly rare but very difficult to find, and all three "chickens": Ruffed, Sharp-tailed and Spruce Grouse, a feat rarely accomplished in one day. Giddy with the successes of the day, I decided that we should report the three Grouse as "Grice!" It's the unanticipated things like these that can happen on a bird trip and make it especially pleasurable and rewarding.

So, while finding a rare bird is usually a peak experience for a birder, it's not the only pleasure that birding provides. People often ask me, sometimes rudely, what do you get out of birding? Or they'll ask me why I'm a birder—as if it's unmanly or uncool. Or what specifically makes birding enjoyable? This book is a series of indirect answers to those questions. I hope non-birders will get a glimpse of what makes birders tick. Wannabe birders will get an idea of what they can expect. Birders will recognize and enjoy experiences and habits they can surely relate to.

Although happiness is in the title, this is not a self-help book—at least not directly. If you flip through it (go ahead!), you won't find any graphs, ten-point action plans, or goopy-eyed cartoon waifs providing slick formulas for boosting you out of whatever "slough of despond" you're stuck in. Birding has provided me with many happy occasions throughout my life, but I'm not presumptuous enough to set out guidelines for achieving happiness in life through birding.

Nor is this book a bird guide or an instructional manual. So there are no photos or drawings of birds (save one by my late wife) and no recommendations for how to improve your bird-spotting identification skills. I'm no ornithologist, professional photographer, or world-recognized birder. I'm a writer who enjoys birding; I've been a sort-of birder since primary school and a writer since my teens. Many of these essays originated as expansions on notes to myself written in journals I've been keeping since 1968. (My previous journals were thrown out by my parents along with a soup box full of bubble gum cards, now worth thousands—the cards, not the journals!) Every Christmas, I'd buy myself a gift: a daybook or journal for the following year to jot down various daily observations, story ideas, trip reports of tours and outings, and reminiscences. Several years ago, I was asked to contribute a monthly blog to a series of nature apps. I ended up expanding notes from my journals into over one hundred blog entries on all nature topics. I've culled some of those blogs about birds and rewritten and expanded them for this book. And I've added more.

As a brief answer to queries about the attractiveness of birding (I prefer that term to the old one, birdwatching, which to me is too passive and smacks of the voyeuristic), I tell people it's like art appreciation. Birds are mobile works of art. You can marvel at their brilliant colours, the pleasing, often abstract arrangement of those colours, the strange, exotic designs, the textures and iridescence. But birds are also aerial acrobats. Watch the frenetic movements of warblers as they search for food and you can't help but be mesmerized. Or follow a hummingbird as it hovers effortlessly above a blossom and speedily reverses away from it, and you will be captivated. Or gaze at two eagles grasping talons high in the air and free-falling in romantic playfulness, and you'll never forget it. I should also mention bird song, so glorious and memorable that many composers have used bird melodies in their music.

But for me, birding is not just about the birds you find, it's also about the people you meet, the places you visit, the experiences you have—the added attractions. Birding has taken me to places as divergent as Churchill, Manitoba and the Galápagos, The Alps and Hawaii, Trinidad and Reykjavik, Texas and Kenya. I've traipsed along the familiar tourist routes and ventured far off those well-beaten paths. I've not just been to Quito, Ecuador but also the Andes and the Amazon rainforests. I was an unsuspecting gawker at the edge of a tear-gassed crowd in Rio and out in the forbidding Pantanal. I've walked the jammed streets of Hanoi and trekked through the cloud-high mountains of Vietnam. Birding is about the stories that you bring back to your daily life and circle of friends from places like this. And that's what this book is about. It's about sharing bird stories.

The first section of the book is about birds that are not so rare but are underappreciated, or even scorned. Sparrows and chickadees, Mallards and crows are so familiar they're taken for granted. Watching them more carefully through the eyes of my grandson after watching them casually for so many years has goaded me into reading about them and thinking about what I might write. When I was a teenager, I used to binge-read the works of authors I liked. After *Walden*, I read everything I could get my hands on by Henry David Thoreau, an idol I'll never live up to. Over the years, I've read everyone from Ernest Thompson Seton (who wrote the original *Birds of Manitoba*) to Kenn Kaufman as well as the binge-worthy Bernd Heinrich and Peter Matthiessen, two other favourites. My portraits are a bit different from theirs because mine are about experiencing the birds and some other people's responses to them, not just descriptions of their looks and behaviours.

Section two focusses on a small fraction of the rare birds that I've been privileged to see in my life. I've seen many rare birds right here in Manitoba and Canada. I've also been fortunate enough to be able to travel to many countries around the world. Often on a trip to a conference or a research library, I'd tack on a few days of birding as a reward for my hard work. On family holidays, I'd reserve some time for birding. And now that I'm retired, I've taken some trips that are mainly dedicated to birding, or birding and culture. If I were to recount my interactions with all the rare birds I've seen and made notes of, this might be a book as long as Karl Ove Knausgaard's recent tome *My Struggle* (3,600 pages, one million words). Be grateful that I'm more laconic than Karl.

In the third section I recount some of the peak experiences I've had as a birder. Birding involves not just planned excursions but a good deal of serendipity, luck. I've been patient (on occasion) and fortunate enough to have had many once-in-a-lifetime, unduplicatable experiences. Chance encounters, unexpected occurrences punctuate my life with bold-faced exclamation points! Some of them have been truly astonishing, some amusing, some scary. All of them have opened my eyes to the glorious variety of nature and the wonders that the world holds.

Finally, I devote some pages to the things that I've encountered that make me grumpy. Birding is not all hummingbirds and pussy willows. There are things I wish I could change. I mention a few in the fourth, but I follow up with portraits of people who counter-act the unhappiness that I sometimes feel. Most of all, birding has introduced me to lots of people who like the things I like and want to do the things I do. That is immensely satisfying. This is a book written in gratitude to them.

Happiness is a rare thing. To paraphrase Emily Dickinson's poem "Hope," happiness, for me, is the thing with feathers.

—*Gene Walz*

Happiness is a Rare Bird

Even Common Birds Can Be Special

House Sparrows
Basic, Economy-sized Birds

"Oh, it's just another House Sparrow!" People say this all the time in mock or real dismay or even profanity-laden disgust. They're usually looking for less common, "more interesting" birds like Lincoln's Sparrows or Lapland Longspurs. House Sparrows, those small, chirpy birds with brown backs and dirty-white underparts that you often see in outdoor cafés and parks, get no respect. (They are the Rodney Dangerfields of the birding world.)

This bad reputation is not entirely undeserved. They are, after all, like pigeons and starlings, rather drab interlopers naively imported into the Americas and other places around the world. (Some birders call them "Euro-trash.") In most of these places they now outnumber more colourful native birds. They are among the original invasive species (if you don't count humans as invasive).

I remember once being told by someone with the mistaken self-assurance of Cliff Clavin (the hilariously misinformed postal worker on the hit TV series *Cheers*) that House Sparrows were brought to New York to eat the horse manure off city streets (as inexpensive, winged street cleaners). Someone else proposed that they were introduced because some romantic soul wanted all the birds mentioned in Shakespeare's plays to be resident in the New World (as ornithological ambassadors of the bard—bard-birds). These two charming "origin" myths have been thoroughly debunked.

Nowadays, House Sparrows are just plain nuisances to many. Around a bird feeder they can act like obnoxious teenagers in front of a convenience store. They're noisy, they're messy, and they're quarrelsome, bullying other birds away from the birdseed. The males, at times, strut around like perfect, feathered gangstas. And when they strop their bills on a branch, they look like they're preparing for battle.

They are also unconscionable nesting box invaders. The Purple Martin housing complex at FortWhyte Alive in Winnipeg is now inhabited by House Sparrows. Bluebirds, wrens, and Tree Swallows have also been ousted from their nest boxes by hostile House Sparrow takeovers.

Wherever they call home, House Sparrows usually make big, ugly nests that are agglomerations of convenient materials—grass, straw, twigs, pieces of plastic bags and wrappers, string, whatever. That's because they are misnamed (part of their charm, perhaps). They're not sparrows at all, but finches. It used to be thought that they were directly related to the Weaver Finches of Africa. That seems unlikely. Weaver Finches construct careful and elaborate nests; House Sparrows can't or aren't interested in painstakingly weaving together sticks and grasses into neat, symmetrical, gourd-like homes. They are messy, careless (or carefree) finches—distant relatives of their African weavers. (A special bone in their tongue, used to make seed-shucking easier and not present in Weaver Finches, rules out a close kinship.)

If you don't like PDA (Public Displays of Affection), you'll not like House Sparrows; they are the birds you are most likely to see copulating. Prepare for it: your young daughter or your grandson will ask about their behaviour at the most inopportune time. What are those birdies doing, Daddy/Grandpa?

Years ago, I met an old Scotsman who maintained a well-stocked bird feeder in his yard in the riparian area of Winnipeg along the Seine River. I recruited him as a feeder observer in my zone of the Christmas bird count. When I delivered the forms for the count, he'd invite me in for a dram of scotch and then regale me with stories of his days in the merchant marine. He was a "wee laddie," maybe five foot four, but his wrists and forearms were the size of two-by-fours. And he smoked a corncob pipe that gave his Scottish burr a gruff edge. I always came away from his house humming, "I'm Popeye the Birding Man."

It always struck me as odd that "Popeye" never had any House Sparrows at his feeders. Everybody else did. So I asked him one year: "Don't you ever get any House Sparrows?" "Aye," he said, "but I shoot 'em!"

Thus the fate of the lowly House Sparrow. Scorned even by supposed bird-lovers.

Popeye the Birding Man soon went on to the great steamship in the sky, but he must be happy up there, knowing that House Sparrow populations are declining here in Winnipeg and across North America.

Twenty years ago we regularly got about 20,000 House Sparrows on our Winnipeg Christmas counts, give or take the two or three or ten that Popeye shot. Our high was 1989 when Winnipeg had the largest count ever recorded in Canada—23,761. Now we're lucky to get five or six thousand.

Lots of factors can account for the decline, or the apparent decline, diseases and far less spillage of grain in the CN railyards east of Winnipeg being the main factors. All I know is that I'll miss them if they go the way of the Passenger Pigeon—from the most numerous to the ranks of the extirpated.

Their "cheep, cheep, cheep" song may be shrill, monotonous, and noisy, but there is something cheery in that chirping, especially on a bitterly cold Manitoba day. It's heartening to know that this hardy bird, the king of the LBJs (little brown jobbies), can maintain a seemingly positive attitude under the worst of winter conditions.

Because they are such hardy birds (they can live to the ripe old age of twenty-five), House Sparrows have managed to gain a foothold on every continent of the world except Antarctica. Everywhere they're found, they've become what Kim Todd, author of the book *Sparrow*, calls "the basic bird, the stripped-down, super-efficiency model."

They may be ubiquitous and common, but they are not ordinary. With their black bibs, grey cheeks, and brown and black feathering, the males are actually quite handsome birds. Maybe if there were far, far fewer of them, if they were much less numerous and as difficult to find as, say, Scarlet Tanagers, those elusive and brilliant red and black birds of the forest, we'd appreciate them more.

Black-capped Chickadees
Cheerful, Little Fluffballs

Chickadees have been my constant companions for the past several winters. On my hour-long dog walks through the southern suburbs of Winnipeg every morning, I've rarely been out of earshot of these little, black-capped, grey and white birds. Even when the wind-chill is minus fifty degrees Celsius, I can hear the familiar arpeggios of these cheery, jittery, little fluffballs.

Chickadees are onomatopoetic birds. The sound of their name describes the bird. Chick-a-dee = the bird. How many birds can you think of that are named for their songs? Not enough, I'm afraid. Jays, of course. Plus Killdeers, phoebes, hummingbirds, Great Kiskadees, pewees, Willets, pipits, Dickcissels, and maybe, in general, warblers (who warble). Imagine for a minute that our forefathers had named other birds for their songs. If robins had been named after their songs, they'd be called Cheerios. Goldfinches would be called Potato Chips.

Chickadees also have the advantage of a musical name that is, thankfully for some, different from its European moniker and one of its American nicknames. Believe it or not, South Carolina rejected the chickadee as its state bird simply because its nickname caused them embarrassment: tit.

Chickadees, of course, don't just sing their names. They add extra "dees" to emphasize the threat level of a situation. And they often drop the "chick" part of the song for an abbreviated, two-descending-note "dee-dee." Sometimes this is extended to four notes: what I interpreted as a kid as "chee-eese-bur-ger."

All birds sing for two primary reasons: to attract a mate and to intimidate rivals. In my walks, I regularly hear what I take to be response calls picking up the lower of the two "dee" sounds, starting with it and adding a second "dee" equally lower. It's as if they are completing a rhyme or singing a short duet. I also hear a high-pitched "dee" and a gargling noise that sounds like it's all x's and n's. Neither of these sounds appear to serve the two primary functions of bird song. Chickadees seem to be "conversing" with each other in what is called "contact calling." Like Canada Geese in flight, they seem to be saying, "I'm here. Where are you? Find anything good to eat? Me neither. See any predators? Hope not." Etc.

Probably more significant are the sounds I can't hear. Much as we appreciate their songs, chickadees don't sing for us. Our ears aren't sophisticated enough for all their notes and tonalities.

Experienced birders can easily distinguish a chickadee's song from one by a White-throated Sparrow, for instance. But how many of us can recognize the difference between urban chickadees and rural ones? According to Bridget Stutchbury, ornithology professor and author of *The Bird Detective: Investigating the Secret Lives of Birds*, urban birds have adapted their vocalizations to cope with the ambient noise of the city. Their songs are louder and shorter. She also reveals that birds that hatch first sing better and are therefore more attractive as mates than their siblings.

Stutchbury's book is full of interesting details like this. She has assembled the findings of bird researchers from around the world. What she doesn't cover and what is only now being investigated are chickadees' other intriguing gifts.

Several years ago, after a vicious winter snowfall, I decided that it was time to be a conscientious bird food provider again. I filled my feeders over a weekend, all six of them, with suet, peanuts, black and striped sunflower seeds, niger, and millet.

Within minutes of stoking the feeders, chickadees began flitting in, grabbing a seed, and flitting away. Not more than ten or fifteen minutes later, all of my usual suspects had arrived: House Sparrows, of course, plus Downy and Hairy Woodpeckers, Blue Jays, House Finches, White-breasted Nuthatches, and, new for the year, Red-breasted Nuthatches.

How did the chickadees know when to show up, and so quickly? What senses did they employ to discover this new source of food? Were there sentries around somewhere that *saw* me filling the feeders and remembered that I'm usually a pretty reliable provider? Did they *hear* me noisily working at the feeders? Or did they *smell* the seeds and zero in on them via their olfactory senses?

We don't often think of birds as having a sense of smell. But recent genomic and brain studies have shown that the sense of smell is much more important in birds than previously thought. The standard wisdom now is that some bird species can use their sense of smell to navigate, forage, or even distinguish individuals. Birds as diverse as sparrows, chickens, pigeons, ducks, shearwaters, albatrosses, and vultures are able to smell. Rails, cranes, grebes, and nightjars as well.

Chickadees are such resourceful little birds with such adaptable brains that I'm not surprised that they were the first to show up. Smell may have lured them in. I'm just glad they showed up.

As for the others, I'm left to wonder: is there a "universal bird language" for food, a sort of avian Esperanto? Do birds communicate with one another to share food info, not just chickadee to fellow chickadees, but chickadee to nuthatches, and finches, and woodpeckers?

Of course, birds hear each other's songs and calls. Catbirds and mockingbirds imitate the notes and melodies of many other species. And recently in Kildonan Park, a Yellow Warbler was heard imitating an Indigo Bunting, or at least altering its own song enough to respond to it. But can birds interpret other species' songs and calls? That's the question. Can a nuthatch tell when a chickadee is saying "food?"

If so, chickadees are pretty altruistic, sharing little creatures. They don't seem to have that "selfish gene" we're hearing so much about in humans and other animals. They are avian socialists.

We should not be at all surprised at this. Chickadees, after all, can change their brains physically every fall to prepare themselves for the different rigors of surviving the cold northern winter. They are remarkable little birds.

Mallards
and Other Tippy Ducks

Every morning at eleven o'clock, five Mallards march out of an elevator at the luxury Peabody Hotel in Memphis, Tennessee, waddle inelegantly across the lobby on a red carpet, hop up three steps, and plunk themselves into a black marble fountain. Their procession is accompanied by the "King Cotton" march by John Philip Sousa. Hundreds of curious tourists watch and giggle. It has to be the funniest march since the March Hare.

At five o'clock in the afternoon, they tumble obediently out of the fountain, trundle back across the red carpet, and take the elevator up to their $200,000 rooftop penthouse, the Duck Palace.

Every time I think about this odd ritual, I laugh. Then again, I laugh at all ducks. To me, ducks are a source of endless amusement. Ducks make me laugh out loud. Of course, cartoon ducks like Daffy (see *Duck Amuck*) or Donald (see *The Band Concert*) um ... quack me up. But *real* ducks do too. *All* ducks, not just "odd ducks"—because all ducks are odd. Maybe it's their French name: canard. Definition of canard—"a groundless rumour." Of course they're groundless. They're usually in the water! (I've always thought that the name for a group of Mallards should be "a rumour of ducks.")

Sometimes in the winter—after most of them have sensibly departed for the south—I forget just how funny ducks are. (Hundreds of them stick around the open spots on our rivers or in the unfrozen areas of the Charleswood Sewage Lagoons.) When they migrate back to Manitoba in

April and May, they bring back to my iced-over mind temporarily forgotten amusements. Ducks are especially funny if they come back early and try to land on frozen ponds. Poor things. They glide in towards the ice and then: Bam. Slide. Flail! They resuscitate deep-down duck laughter.

Especially amusing are the puddle ducks (because they hang out in puddles and small ponds) also called dabblers (because they nibble and dabble on algae and weeds). These dabbling or puddle ducks—Mallards and wigeons and teal and the like—don't walk or run, they waddle, and when they waddle, they wag their stumpy, little duck tails behind them.

When they're hungry, they plunk their heads under water and stick those same duck tails straight up in the air—to show us why Elvis Presley's haircut was called a DA. When he was four, this move made my grandson Torsten laugh, and there's nothing more contagious than a four-year-old's giggles.

Torsten called them tippy ducks—because they tip over and show their bums. (Bums are especially fascinating and amusing to pre-schoolers.) In my neck of the woods there are eight species of tippy ducks: the Northern Pintail (*Anas acuta*), Gadwall (*Anas strepera*), American Wigeon (*Anas americana*), Northern Shoveler (*Anas clypeata*), Black Duck (*Anas rubripes*), Green-winged Teal (*Anas crecca*), Blue-winged Teal (*Anas discors*), and, of course, the most familiar of them all, the Mallard (*Anas platyrhynchos*). In the pond at St. Vital Park we have watched Gadwalls gad about, wigeons wige, shovelers shovel, and Mallards waddle and paddle for breadcrumbs tossed by kids and misguided grandparents.

This group of ducks only rarely dives. Compared to diving ducks, which have large feet and smaller wings to facilitate underwater swimming, dabblers have larger wings and small feet more centrally located on their bellies. These features allow dabblers to spring straight up from the water and fly strongly away from danger. Diving ducks need to scamper across the water for a short distance to gain momentum for takeoff.

Dabblers are great ducks for initiating pre-schoolers into the practice of recognizing and identifying birds. With their distinctive colours and shapes, they are not too much of a challenge to identify. They're also gregarious, they frequent shallow waters in parks and marshes, and their ability to shoot up and out of the water makes them easier to approach.

Other ducks that must run along the water to get airborne spook much more easily and don't allow a person to get too close.

Tippy ducks also make funny, easy to imitate noises. I taught my grandson how to say "rant" through his nose and in the back of his mouth. It's the perfect duck sound (unlike the simple "quack" that ordinary folks use, or Mel Blanc's Daffy Duck voice, or Clarence Nash's Donald Duck voice). Coming from a four-year-old with a falsetto voice, the "rant" sounded like a cross between a rubber squeaky toy and an actual duck. Nothing funnier than that!

Only nine now, I'll wait a while until I surprise Torsten with another funny thing about ducks. Male ducks have external penises. Most birds don't. Of the 10,000 species of birds in the world, only three percent have penises: ducks, geese, swans, ostriches, and emus. And some ducks have weirdly shaped penises as long as their bodies. Funny thing is, it's only recently that people have noticed.

Nuthatches and Woodpeckers
Birds with Sticky Feet

Young eyes and young minds can bring entirely fresh perspectives to any endeavor.

A babysitting grandma recently brought her five-year-old granddaughter to an early-May bird outing. As we walked along a woody path, a Brown Creeper landed at the base of a bare Manitoba maple tree not more than five feet away from us. The little girl marvelled as the aptly named bird slowly crept up one side of the tree trunk. Rather than blending in with the bark, it presented a distinctive puffball silhouette, its white belly a perfect contrast to the dull brown background.

It was so close and so deliberate in its movements, we could all see its slightly de-curved bill. The girl's grandma softly noted that it was probing for insects to eat. And she mentioned that it was using its stiff tail feathers to keep it from toppling over backwards. Finally the girl whispered, "It's got sticky feet!"

That childlike description reminded me of my grandson when he saw his first White-breasted Nuthatch, another bird with sticky feet. Circling downward on a tree trunk, the grey and white nuthatch was hard to miss, even by young, inexperienced eyes. I told him it was called a nuthatch, thinking he'd be as amused by the word as I was when I was his age. On the spot he made up his own name: Upside-down Bird. Perfect.

Nuthatches probably got him hooked on birds. Often they came to my bird feeders, quickly grabbed a sunflower seed, and flitted off to eat it in solitude or cache it for later. After a while he started to recognize their peculiar call: a soft, nasal "wank" or "nert." (A friend's grandchildren call them "nert-nerts.") Whenever he heard it, he'd head for the spot where he thought the call came from.

From nuthatches, he moved on to woodpeckers. Unlike nuthatches, they sit upright on tree trunks and branches. But they too seem to have sticky feet. Tapping and calling from higher up in trees, they're usually harder to find—unless there's a suet or peanut feeder handy. When they attack a suet ball, they can be even more acrobatic than nuthatches. One Downy Woodpecker regularly visits my feeders, hanging from the bottom and tapping upward to get each morsel of suet or peanut shard.

Once, I was lucky enough to spot a Hairy Woodpecker within a couple of feet of a Downy. The distinctions between the two—the Hairy is larger with a bigger bill and a sharper, louder call—were lost on my grandson, but he quickly learned to identify two other members of the woodpecker family—a Yellow-shafted Flicker (bigger and tawnier than the black and white Downies and often found on the ground hunting for ants) and a Yellow-bellied Sapsucker (a little harder to distinguish unless it's near a series of small holes it drills for sap).

I've resisted the urge to instruct my grandson in the finer points of bird-talon anatomy. He doesn't need to know the differences between three-toed and four-toed woodpeckers or the remarkable way they can lock their talons into tree bark and sleep away an entire night without letting go. TMI, as they say: Too Much Information for a kid.

Years ago I helped produce an instructional birding video for kids. I now realize how misguided that video is. We went at it backwards; we did it from an adult's point of view. If I were allowed a do-over, I'd present it from a kid's perspective, with categories like Lawn Birds (robins, crows, flickers, et al.), Floaters (ducks and geese), Hyper Birds (warblers and hummingbirds), Rainbow Birds (red ones, blue ones, yellows, and greens), Little Brown Jobbies (sparrows, wrens, et al.), Hunters (raptors and owls), and Sticky Feet Birds. And I'd encourage kids to make up their own bird names, taxonomies, and stories.

My grandson now lives in Europe. He moved there before I could show him one of my favourite Sticky Feet Birds—the Red-headed Woodpecker. It's disappeared from my suburban St. Vital neighbourhood; in fact, it's almost impossible to find anywhere in Winnipeg nowadays.

People in general, and city-officials in particular, don't like to leave dead trees standing around for long, fearful of possible lawsuits should they fall on someone's head. Redheads need open areas (like golf courses and city parks) with dead trees to nest in. They're gone.

I miss the orioles and Mourning Doves that used to hang out in my neighbourhood, victims of other human incursions. But most of all, I miss the woodpeckers with their bold black and white bodies and stunning red heads.

In Europe, my grandson has already identified Green, Black, and Great Spotted Woodpeckers, three fairly common species with sticky feet. They had him running to his bird guide.

Someday I hope to show him a Pileated Woodpecker—a crow-sized, dramatically black and white bird with a red crest. Or I'll take him to the American southwest to see the wonderful Acorn Woodpeckers there. I'm sure he'll love their clownish faces and their acorn-storing habits. If we want the younger generations to appreciate nature, there's no better way than showing them the upside-down birds or the birds with sticky feet.

A Great Blue Heron
Returns Before Ice-out

We'll never really understand bird migration. Recent studies have shown that routes and times are instinctive—inherited in a bird's DNA. But what about the early birds? The cliché says they "get the worm." What about the ones who seem to have completely mis-timed their arrival in spring?

I'm reminded of this early in April, when birds return while the lakes and ponds and streams are still rock-stiff with ice, and snow still covers the ground in thick white drifts and patches. Those birds brave or foolish enough to return to Manitoba when there's still snow on the ground shine in the sky as if they are lit from within—and lit with a 500-watt bulb. The sun reflecting off the snow turns raptors and geese into stunning bird-ghosts, their white undersides brighter than bright as they wing overhead.

Even birds that don't have white undersides can look white. In early April a couple of years ago, a Great Blue Heron flew over me as I was raptor-spotting on the St. Adolphe Bridge. It shone so brightly that for a second I thought it might be a white morph (Great White Heron) or an intermediate (Wurdeman's Heron). A closer look revealed its silvery blue feathers shining like a brand new quarter.

Great Blue Herons like this one look so relaxed, so laid-back when they fly that I sometimes wonder just how they stay aloft. The wings beat slowly and steadily. The long neck is not determinedly stretched out straight in front like cranes or geese; it coils back on itself in a kind of lazy slouch.

If herons in flight seem lackadaisical, there is something both elegant and goofy about them when they walk. They remind me of John Cleese in Monty Python doing a slow motion "silly walk." When I think of evolutionary biology, I always wonder which came first: the heron's neck or its legs. Is its neck so long so it can reach its food? Or are its legs so long because prehistoric herons kept bashing their long beaks on the ground, tripping over them, and snagging them on everything?

Watching that intrepid heron, white as snow, fly slowly over the St. Adophe Bridge that cold April day, I had no idea how the premature migrant was going to find food. The rivers were still frozen two feet thick. A long, cold winter meant that marshes and streams would not thaw for a month. Who knows how long it would take before the fish and frogs and slugs and bugs that suit a heron's palate made an appearance.

Once the ice melts and the heron's food supplies make an appearance, this bird stalks its prey with the proverbial patience of Job. It stiffens into a feathered statue, its bill and long neck poised like a javelin. Then it springs!

As I followed that too-early, too-eager heron as it flew past, all I could do was wonder. I knew that an early heron gets the best breeding and feeding spots. But if it were to try hunting for food, it would shatter its bill into a million splinters and end up with a very sore neck. I wanted to shout, "It's still winter up here, dummy. I hope you've got a good reserve of fat from your warmer wintering ground."

Instead, I turned my attention back to the Bald Eagles and Red-tailed Hawks that were streaming past. It was a day better suited to them. The thermals created by the sunny skies, the snow cover, and the exposed fields made it easy for them to soar and glide towards their northern destinations. And they have diets better suited to the cold than the heron does. Just thinking about them made me feel cold and hungry. I needed to get out of the wind and get a good bowl of soup in me. Once the heron was out of sight, my April birding was done for the day.

American White Pelicans
Ghost Riders in the Sky

People often see what they want to see and hear what they hope to hear. It's one of the hazards of birding. Wishin' and hopin' to find a rare bird can sometimes lead to embarrassing misidentifications. It's called confirmation bias. I've done it myself. Most of my betters have too.

There's a famous story about iron-willed British Prime Minister Margaret Thatcher in this regard. At a meeting, she once claimed to have heard a Nightingale singing on a February night outside her prime ministerial residence at Ten Downing Street. An underling meekly challenged her identification skills by pointing out that Nightingales migrated to Africa in winter.

When Maggie insisted that she could not have been mistaken, the underling tried to suggest other possibilities—until his boss, a cabinet minister, took him outside and sharply castigated him. "If the prime minister says she heard a Nightingale in February, then by Jove she heard a Nightingale!"

We don't have any amateur birders in Manitoba with quite the clout of Maggie Thatcher, but almost every spring or fall, people report seeing Whooping Cranes here. It's highly unlikely, but not impossible. Whooping Cranes have been known to stray from their normal migratory route from Northern Alberta and the Northwest Territories to the Texas coast and back. They have been positively confirmed here, but not very often. (I was with a large group of birders who saw one south of St. Adolphe.)

More likely what people see are American White Pelicans. In the air, pelicans can look surprisingly similar to Whoopers. Both have white bodies and wings and black wing extremities. If they get too excited about seeing a rare Whooper, people might mistake the pelican's long bill for the crane's long neck, and they don't notice the absence of the crane's long, trailing legs.

People don't expect to see pelicans in Manitoba. They think pelicans are ocean or coastal dwellers. That's the Brown Pelican, a more colourful, if less elegant, bird. In fact, White Pelicans are pretty numerous on Manitoba's lakes and rivers—so numerous that they are periodically slaughtered by fishermen who erroneously believe that pelicans and cormorants are responsible for fish-stock depletions.

Pelicans are among my favourite local birds. To see a dozen of them appearing, disappearing, and magically reappearing as they soar in languid arcs high above a prairie lake can distract me even when I'm fiercely concentrating on a golf green. It happens almost every time I play the ninth hole at Clear Lake Golf Course. They hardly seem to move their wings at all. Appearing and disappearing, like ghost riders in the sky.

Watching a small group as it works together to herd fish, grab them, and lets them wriggle in their rubbery bill pouches can make the kid in me rise again to the surface. At Lockport, Manitoba, I once marvelled as a pelican caught a fish in its bill that seemed far too large to fit down its throat and into its belly. It took ten or twelve tries, but the pelican finally tilted its head back and slid the live, wriggling fish down its throat. The fish was twice as wide as the pelican's neck, but somehow the neck didn't burst wide open. Amazing!

I'm in good company in my fascination with pelicans, and misidentifiers are not alone in their mistakes. The famous Greek philosopher Aristotle "studied" them and concluded that pelicans swallowed clamshells whole, cooked them in their pouches, and then vomited them up to feed on the exposed and cooked flesh. The pelicans cooked and shelled the clams in their pouches without the aid of a stove, clam knife, or plyers. Hmmm!

Great philosopher, Aristotle. Terrible ornithologist!

Eyeball to Eyeball
with a Short-eared Owl

The first time I ever saw a Short-eared Owl, it was flying at eye level about ten feet from my car window as I drove along the west edge of Oak Hammock Marsh north of Winnipeg. I was with my good friend Lew Layman, a guy who loves owls. We were both gob-smacked as it turned its head slightly and stared right at us with its big, yellow eyes. And, instead of flapping away, it stayed with my car at about twenty miles per hour for several minutes. Only ten feet away. It instantly became my favourite owl.

Thinking back on it, I wish my grandson had been with me then. He would have enjoyed the "race" between a car and an owl, one of his favourite birds. Who was leading whom? Was I in the pace car or was it the pace owl?

Because it was so close and stuck with us so long, I was able to get a great read on its markings. Medium-sized, tawny colour with white belly and under-wings, and a streaky breast. The head had a beige facial disk and the yellow eyes were surrounded by black—as if it were wearing mascara. Mascara—my grandson would have loved that image!

The distinctive flight would surely have fascinated him. There's nothing that compares. It truly does remind you of the flight of a moth. It beats its long, floppy wings in an unhurried, irregular way, occasionally dipping to one side or another as it hunts low to the ground for voles and mice and other small rodents.

Then you realize: hey, it's ten o'clock in the morning, and I'm eyeball to eyeball with an owl! Another reason to like it. It's one of very few owls that are diurnal; it hunts during daylight hours. It also hunts like other owls, at night (nocturnal), but your best bet to see them is to look at dawn and dusk (crepuscular).

Not long after that encounter I saw about twenty Short-eared Owls over the course of a couple of hours in the very same place—Oak Hammock Marsh. That can happen. Occasionally they flock together when the hunting is good. I've not been as lucky since. All birding involves a certain amount of serendipity.

But I have been lucky enough to see Short-eared Owls in all four seasons. My second best sighting happened on a Christmas Bird Count, the annual census of all the birds within a twelve-mile circle. The wind was howling across the bald-headed prairie, and Lew, Andy Courcelles, another birding friend, and I weren't finding anything. Our census list was pathetic—some chickadees, a few nuthatches, a Downy Woodpecker or two, some House Sparrows. Most birds were in hiding, hunkered down out of the wind. So we stopped at a short bridge across an irrigation ditch to see if any Rock Pigeons were taking shelter there. That's how desperate we were; hunting for pigeons to bulk up our census list. We were desperate to find anything at all.

Suddenly, three large, tawny birds boomed out from the cramped space. Grouse? No! Three Short-eared Owls! And boy, did they look mad at us for chasing them from their warm hiding place! Lew, owl aficionado and shameless punster, exclaimed, "Irritable Owl Syndrome, I think."

No moth-like fluttering by these three owls. They took off as if they had turbo-boosters. Racing side by side with them was out of the question. They headed across a snow-covered, bumpy stubble-field and were quickly out of sight.

How'd we know they were Short-eared Owls? We'd each caught enough of a glimpse of them to be sure of their identity: tawny colour, white underneath, yellow eyes, and, oh, no "ears," the ornamental tufts of feathers that distinguish them from Long-eared Owls.

If it weren't so silly, I'd suggest that they be re-named. Maybe No-eared Owls. But even my grandson knows an owl's ears are beneath their feathers. Ears are one of their unseen, dominant features. Maybe Moth-like Owls would be a better moniker.

Because of these three owls, seen in this area on a Christmas count for the first time ever, we ended up with the best list at the tally dinner. The others birders just smiled when we listed them as No-eared Owls.

Merlins
and Other Bird Brains

My friend Harry has been complaining about the Merlins in his south Winnipeg neighbourhood for years. These smallish, brown (female) or grey (male) falcons have nested in his evergreens, terrorizing the birds at his feeders. And they're noisy birds; their shrill, piercing "key, key, key" calls, especially during nesting season, only add to their nuisance quotient.

Harry would love to shoot them, but there are city bylaws. And lately he says that he's gained a new, grudging respect for them. They're smarter than he originally thought.

He wonders whether they may have adopted a new hunting tactic. Instead of catching birds on the wing, the Merlins have been scaring their prey into flying, panic-stricken, into his picture windows and then feasting on them after they've stunned themselves and fallen onto the ground. Smart birds! Easy pickings, minimal effort.

I didn't know quite what to think until I saw a female Merlin in my own yard, miles away from Harry's, doing the same thing. I was standing over the sink in my kitchen when I heard a soft thump on my patio doors. Quickly checking to find out what made the sound, I discovered a Merlin casually retrieving its unconscious prey. She was mantling a sparrow (stretching her wings out to prevent other possible predators from seeing and poaching it), but from my covert vantage point, I had a good look.

In short order, the sparrow's feathers were flying. The Merlin removed the head and gorged herself on the bird's torso. Within five minutes, all that was left were the separated wings, the head and tail, and a pile of downy feathers. Nature, in the poet Tennyson's phrase, "red in tooth and claw"—or beak and claw.

I was still skeptical of the apparent cleverness of the Merlins after my sighting. One or two examples were hardly scientific. Was the tactic planned? Did the Merlins calculate and then execute a strategy? Or were they just lucky? When I recounted these stories to some friends, one of them asked me whether any other birds qualified as smart. I tossed his question back at him, using the tried and true professorial gambit.

He took a minute and then offered, hesitantly: robins?

Surprised, I asked him why he chose robins.

"I don't know much about birds," he stammered, "but I've read that bird populations are declining rapidly. But I see robins all the time. I figure they must be smart enough, adaptable enough, to buck the trends."

I told him that robins first adapted their behaviour hundreds of years ago. Before white settlement of North America and especially before the middle class obsession with lush, extensive lawns, robins were forest dwellers. They especially liked the open, green spaces of forests recently cleared by forest fires. They've learned to co-exist with people, hunting for worms and grubs on suburban lawns and building mud nests on and near houses. They're smarter than people think.

Examples of brainy birds, of birds adapting to changing conditions, are not difficult to find. Think of Barn Owls and Barn Swallows and Chimney Swifts. They all existed in North America before barns and chimneys were built. They were smart enough to adapt—to examine a situation, imagine an alternative way of living, and change their behaviour. And adaptation continues. There's evidence that Barn Swallows have learned to fly through the scanners that trigger the automatic door openers that allow them to get into and out of Big Box home and garden stores. Nesting inside is easier than nesting out in the weather.

Other smart birds? Parrots come quickly to mind. If you've read the book *Tuco: The Parrot, the Others, and a Scattershot World* by Brian Brett, you already know that parrots aren't just great mimics, they're also highly intelligent and sensitive creatures, capable of empathy, cruelty, and humor. Some people have suggested that eagles are really smart; I don't know why. Believe it or not, others have voted for Canada Geese, but that just seems ignorant to me.

Like many conversations, this one ended in mid-air. I never did get to provide the ultimate answer: the smartest birds in the world are the corvids—ravens, crows, jays, magpies, and nutcrackers. But that was a story for another day.

Corvids
The Smartest Birds in the World

My first bird book was *The Golden Nature Guide to Birds*. It was printed in 1949, but I didn't get my copy until 1952 or 1953. Before then, I birded without the benefit of binoculars or a book. I guess I was engaged in close-quarter ornithological research without even knowing what the words meant. I had plenty of time on my hands (this was before computers and TV dominated kids' free time) to stake out a birdy spot and wait for whatever came along. It could take hours.

Before I got the *Golden Guide,* I only knew the names of very common birds: robin, chickadee, pheasant, pigeon, Mallard, etc. For some others, I didn't make fine distinctions: all owls were Hoot Owls, Goldfinches were wild canaries, all gulls were simply seagulls. For the rest, I had to make up my own names. The only ones I can now remember are "Chatterbox" for the Warbling Vireo and "Sad Bird" for the Mourning Dove. I wish I'd kept the lists I created as a ten-year-old.

The *Golden Guide* was skimpy. It covered only 112 birds—"The Most Familiar American Birds." For instance, it had crow but not raven. For a while I thought they were the same bird—just like puma and cougar describes the same animal. After I read Edgar Allen Poe, I thought I had to listen for the raven's song "Nevermore" to tell the difference. I figured "Nevermore" was a transcription of the bird's song into English, like "Old Sam Peabody, Peabody, Peabody" was the mnemonic for the White-throated Sparrow's song, and "Pleased, pleased, pleased to meetcha" a transcription of the Chestnut-sided Warbler's song, and "Drink your tea" what the Eastern Towhee "says."

I can trace my fascination with corvids back to those early days of birding. There's something about these big, jet-black birds with their blunt, noisy calls that always catches my attention—wherever they are.

Like in the Bible. A raven is the first bird mentioned in the Bible—in the flood story in Genesis 8: 6–12. After forty days, "Noah sent forth a raven and a dove." The dove returned shortly, tired and bedraggled, not having found dry land. The raven is never again mentioned. It seems to have disappeared into thin air. Presumed dead, I guess.

I've often wondered: Whatever happened to that raven? Did it succumb or was it just stronger and smarter than the dove? After forty days cooped up in a home-built, DIY ark with two of every other species in the world, the liberated raven probably vowed to find refuge somewhere, anywhere, or die trying. (Imagine the noise, the smells, the crowded quarters, and resulting Darwinian animosities in that ark!) Smart cookie, that first raven. It found a tall, leafless tree and waited a couple of days for its mate to be set free so that they could propagate the species.

Recently, corvids have been studied almost as extensively as the Bible and more so than other bird species. Among the best studies are Bernd Heinrich's *Mind of the Raven* or *Ravens in Winter* or even *A Year in the Maine Woods;* they are brilliantly readable and informative books. For an even broader view, pick up *Bird Brains: The Intelligence of Crows, Ravens, Magpies and Jays* by Candace Savage or *The Genius of Birds* by Jennifer Ackerman.

Corvids have enormous brains relative to their size. Some ornithologists consider crows and ravens equal in brain capacity and power to apes and dolphins. As the three above authors point out, corvids are capable of designing and using tools and of giving gifts. They are smart and social and playful. Pigeons and geese are social; they hang out together. But they don't seem to completely understand the full implications of cooperation and competition to the extent that crows and ravens do. Crows, for instance, often have "nesting assistants"—a third crow at the nest that aids in feeding and protecting a brood.

And though pigeons and geese fly in groups, they don't seem to enjoy flying, to be as playful in flight as crows and ravens. Corvids take delight in the wind; they perform with it. I've watched them swooping and soaring and somersaulting for the pure joy of it. This playfulness, this exuberance, inspires me. It makes me jealous, stirs my soul, exhilarates me. Corvids' playfulness, to me, is a true sign of their intelligence.

Corvids not only possess unusual cognitive abilities, they're also capable of emotion. Bernd Heinrich, listed above and one of my favourite authors and scientists who has studied ravens closely for years, feels that he can "detect a raven's surprise, happiness, bravado, and self-aggrandizement from its voice and body language." They can also be cranky, greedy, affectionate, grieving, and sly.

They are also patient, which to me shows a certain amount of intelligence. One crow watched a Killdeer's nest at FortWhyte Alive and waited patiently for a chick to be born, seeming to prefer it to an egg. As Killdeers are precocious birds, able to scurry into hiding quickly after being born, the crow timed his predation perfectly. It swooped in, grabbed the nestling, and flew off with a meal before the adult Killdeer even noticed.

A couple of years ago, a Winnipeg crow seemed to hold a personal grudge against a postal worker, recognizing him whenever he walked his route and dive-bombing him viciously. I too have been singled out by a neighbourhood crow, angry with me on my daily dog walks. Facial or body recognition and memory are measures of intelligence. It also seemed to have a special call to bring in other crows for possible backup whenever I appeared, perhaps the result of my disturbing its nest the previous year. The racket they made, as if taunting me, was unnerving.

After West Nile fever reduced the numbers of corvids several years ago, they are making a strong comeback. Record numbers of corvids are now being entered in the Winnipeg Christmas bird count. And in my neighbourhood, they are much more numerous than ever before. In the early fall I can count scores of crows streaming northward in the evening for weeks at a time; well over a hundred of them assemble in a nearby park at dusk. A dozen or so regularly hang out at McDonalds.

During the winter, I'm delighted to see crows and ravens. Their dark presence can enliven even the bleakest wintry landscape. In March, if I'm lucky, the ravens will amuse me with their aerial courtship displays. Twisting and diving and swooping, they're marvelous aeronauts. It's still the dead of winter, minus forty degrees, and they're courting and mating. In the air! (Is there a Kamasutra for birds somewhere? Is this part of parental training? Or do they just have vivid imaginations and playful natures?) Amazing birds!

In the spring and summer, however, crows and ravens make me extremely nervous. They're too smart. They'll find and devour eggs, fledglings, and smaller birds. No wonder Kingbirds and Red-winged Blackbirds chase them and dive-bomb them whenever they can. They're brainy menaces, something I too often forget in the winter. With apologies to Edgar Allen Poe, I'd like to see them disappear and, ahem, "nevermore" be seen.

Kathy
and the Pileated Woodpeckers

My wife Kathy's passion for birds did not match my own—though I thought it did when we were courting.

Courting, as some of you may recall, was a quaint and elaborate pre-marital ritual of testing and pleasing your prospective partner to determine whether you were more than temporarily compatible or completely deluded. (It's since been superseded by computer dating and immediate co-habitation.)

When I was writing my PhD thesis, I signed up for a ten-week, non-credit "course" in birdwatching to allow me one sane day per week. The course met at dawn on ten consecutive spring Saturday mornings. Kathy showed up every Saturday at dawn.

I thought I had found a perfect mate: a beautiful, smart, sensible, sensitive woman. BONUS: she too loves birds. It turns out she was my ideal mate for nearly forty years; but she loved a certain birder (me!) more than she loved the birds.

That's not to say that she didn't like birds. She did. But they had to be special, i.e., big, colourful, stationary, and close. The little, flitty ones she didn't have much patience for, no matter how rare, delicately beautiful, or sonorous.

Birds were just one of many things she was interested in: her family, skydiving, camping, travelling, Star Wars paraphernalia, garage sales, gardening, photography, watercolours, wretched soap operas, lighthouses, hot air ballooning, animals of all kinds, a good mystery, the internet, and especially the frail, difficult, and rejected kids that she tended as a school psychologist. The list of her enthusiasms is long.

When she saw Pileated Woodpeckers late in the summer of 2010, she was delighted. Here was her perfect North American bird.

A big, robust bird, eighteen inches long with a huge, 28-inch wingspan, a Pileated Woodpecker is not what you'd call pretty or elegant. In fact, it's somewhat prehistoric-looking. It's got stark, basic colours—a black body and wings, a white face and neck with a black stripe down the nape, and a dashing, thin, black (female) or black and red (male) "moustache" stripe. Its most distinctive feature is its flame-red head, sweeping back rakishly into a tapering point. The bird takes its name from this stunning feature—pileated (either pill-ee-ated or pye-lee-ated is acceptable) meaning "having a crest."

Pileateds are not common birds, but they're not rare either. They are uncommon in more ways than one. They prefer forests with dead trees to drill for food (carpenter ants and beetles) and to hollow out their nest cavities. With long, thick, sturdy chisels for bills, their loud drilling is quite unique—like the sound of a marble-sized steel ball tapping noisily down a wooden set of stairs. That'll get your attention. If not, their piercing, clear, unmistakable call will. It's similar to the loud barking of a small terrier. Ka ka ka ka ka ka kaa! Or a series of whinnying whoops.

Recently, Pileateds have become somewhat more numerous along the rivers in Winnipeg. When I see them, I feel that it's almost a privilege, especially if they come to my yard to peck at my suet feeder or drill into a dead ash or aspen trunk. Huge chips fly everywhere. It's a wonder that they don't give themselves concussions.

I've also seen a pair engaged in a mating dance. They were coyly playing tag, chirping loudly at each other and hopping around a hydro pole and then swooping back and forth to a nearby tree trunk, the female never too far ahead of the male. In their typically undulating woodpecker flight, the large patches of white under their wings made the scene all the more vivid—two or three wingbeats showing their white patches, then they fold the wings close and go into a loop, all in black.

Although I'd seen them often, even in our own yard, my wife had whiffed on them repeatedly for over forty years.

In late summer 2010, we were on a small, hilly island in the middle of Lake Temagami in northern Ontario. Our hosts suggested that there was a spectacular vista on the other side of the island. Although Kathy could barely walk and was in excruciating pain (from what we thought was sciatica but turned out to be bone cancer of her sacrum and femurs), she couldn't resist an opportunity for a mini-adventure or the possibility of a good photograph.

Even in her pain, Kathy somehow got ahead of the rest of us. (We were stopping to look at migrating warblers—her least favourite bird.) When we caught up with her at the top of the island, Kathy was beaming. She showed us what she'd just shot on her digital camera. "My new favourite bird!"

Not just one but three spectacular Pileated Woodpeckers sat calmly on a bare birch tree, just as she had wanted them: big, colourful, stationary, and close. A photograph of them (see page ii) is the last nature photograph she ever took.

Pileated Woodpeckers will always have a special place in my heart.

Rest in peace, my "Lifer" Kathryn Manix Walz
October 16, 1945 – January 20, 2011

What Is So Rare As

Atlantic Puffins
Clowns of the Sea

Puffins aren't at all rare along the Atlantic and Pacific coasts. But for a prairie guy, they're a rare treat.

Atlantic Puffins are odd, stumpy seabirds that look like a mad scientist somehow engineered them out of genetic materials from a penguin, a toucan, a hummingbird, and a football. Perhaps that's why they're called the clowns of the sea. They're funny-looking!

They're also cute—cuter than their Pacific cousins, Horned and Tufted Puffins. They're probably the only bird truly worthy of a plush animal toy. With their black backs, white fronts, and stubby tails, they might be mistaken for foot-tall baby penguins. Except for one thing—their colourful, over-sized beaks! With orange and yellow stripes and a large, sideways, steel-blue triangle, the beaks make a bold contrast with the puffins' sober black and white bodies. Adding to their quirkiness are bright orange feet and what look to be triangular eyes.

If I were a bulkier, shorter person (Danny DeVito, say, who notoriously played a penguin in a Batman movie), I'd consider dressing up like a puffin this Halloween; all it would take is a black tux, white shirt, orange running shoes, and a colourful proboscis.

The best place to see puffins is Iceland. I once got caught in a whirlwind of flying puffins on the top of a cliff on the south side of the island. Hundreds of them flew up from the water, swirled around my wife, Kathy, and me, and then dove back into the sea, coming up with beaks full of tiny fish. It was both thrilling and a bit scary as they almost fetched us over the cliff with them.

Puffins are so plentiful there and fly so close to the volcanic cliffs that Icelanders catch them easily with nets as they fly. Or they knock them out of the air with oars and brooms. Then they cook them and eat them. I couldn't bring myself to a feast of puffin when I was there, but I hear that they are tasty—like chicken (or rattlesnakes). Then again, everything exotic "tastes like chicken."

You don't have to fly halfway across the Atlantic to find them. It's getting easier to watch them off the coast of Maine thanks to Project Puffin, a program begun in the 1970s. At that point in time, puffin nesting-sites in the US were reduced to two small islands north of Bar Harbor, Maine. Dedicated conservationists, alarmed because puffins don't mate until age seven and produce only one egg per year, established two other colonies nearby. Now there are several pelagic tours in the area to take birders out to see the puffins at their breeding grounds. Three 24/7 live feeds from webcams mounted on Maine's Seal Island currently provide intimate views of puffins for those too seasick to risk a boat ride out to see them.

My wife and I had to skip Seal Island. The waters were too choppy for the puffin boats to venture out into the ocean. We hung around in a campsite for three days, waiting for the ocean to calm, the only consolation being the lobster dinners we had every night. The seas might have been too scary for puffin boats, but they didn't prevent the lobsterman who owned our campsite from going out to sea to retrieve his lobster pots every day. In the morning he'd ask us if we wanted lobsters for that evening. Later in the day he'd return with two pound-and-a-half beauties, fresh from the ocean. And at less than half the price we'd have had to pay in a restaurant. We were not too disappointed.

To have a close encounter with puffins in North America, my wife and I had to wait until several summers later when we took a boat from Englishtown, Nova Scotia to Bird Island off the north coast of Cape Breton. There we saw lots of puffins, Razorbills, and Black Guillemots bobbing gently in the waves and flying up to the rocky island to sun themselves. All three birds were new to me in Canada, and they were mere feet away from us. So the wait was well worth it.

All three of these waterfowl are basically black and white seabirds distinguished mainly by their beaks. The Razorbills are mostly black with white undersides and thick, round-tipped bills. The Black Guillemots are mostly black with white wing patches, red feet, and pointy bills that reveal a red mouth when they open them. They're easy to tell apart.

Puffins are especially fun to watch in the air and diving for fish. They have slender wings that allow them to swim underwater like penguins. But the combination of stumpy bodies and short wings means they have to flap their wings faster than any other birds except for hummingbirds. Puffins flap their wings at 300-400 beats per minute, or five to seven times a second—almost, but not quite, like the blur of a hummingbird's wings.

Seeing swarms of puffins buzzing around you or bobbing in the ocean with as many as ten small fish tucked into their beaks is quite a treat. No matter how gloomy you are, watching puffins will definitely cheer you up.

A Gray-crowned Rosy-Finch
Truculent Vagabond

Most die-hard birders keep lists of the birds they see. All kinds of lists: life lists (the total number of birds seen in your lifetime), yearly and even monthly lists, yard lists, daily trip lists, provincial lists, national lists (for Canada and every other country visited—all separate), dead-of-winter lists (for birds seen when Manitoba winters are at their coldest), and on and on. Me? I'm not nearly as thorough (or anal).

I'm most conscientious about my Manitoba list. It stands at 340 species seen by me in the province—out of 400 or so recorded here since records have been kept. So it's getting tougher and tougher for me to add new species to my Manitoba life list. I've seen virtually all of the resident birds found here. I'm lucky if I can add one new bird per year.

Like other birders, I pray for rarities—what the books call "vagrants and accidentals"—birds that aren't supposed to be here. I prefer the term "vagabonds." Adventurous birds or strays whose internal GPSs have gone wonky.

When one shows up, I get all twitchy. I'm not the only one.

That's how I ended up in a car full of birders chasing a Gray-crowned Rosy-Finch that was more than a three-and-a-half hour drive from Winnipeg. It was early January—frigid, the roads were icy, and we left before daylight. A long, potentially dangerous slog for one small bird—and there was no guarantee we'd even get to see it!

Gray-crowned Rosy-Finches breed in arctic and alpine tundra regions in western North America and eastern Asia. According to *The Birds of*

Manitoba, the first one was recorded here in 1891; since then these sturdy little birds have ventured eastward into Manitoba only fifteen times; before our January trip, the last time one was seen here was over twenty years ago. I missed it.

When we got to the remote grasslands farm in western Manitoba, it took less than a minute to spot our target bird. The finch sat in perfect profile, Roger Tory Peterson-style, on the roof of a farmhouse, evidently eating grit from the shingles.

After each of us gave it a thorough examination, the bird flew off, and the homeowners, who had first spotted the bird and notified the birding community, invited us into their house to get warm. They were clearly happy to have the company, had had several car-loads of birders visit them before us, and served us coffee and cookies. Once, when I lived in Massachusetts, a farmer was so incensed at the hordes of birders attracted by a rare Snowy Owl that he shot the owl. These cordial farmers were more the rule than the horrid exception when it came to welcoming birders. Truly friendly Manitobans.

As we chatted, the finch returned and alighted on their bird feeder, less than three feet away through the kitchen window.

Slightly bigger than a sparrow with a yellow beak, a pink wash to its plumage, black legs, and surprisingly long talons, this particular bird, on closer inspection, proved to be the "interior" variety of Gray-crowned Rosy-Finches: *Leucosticte tephrocotis*.

A truculent bird, it not only chased all the House Sparrows away from the feeder, it jumped right into the seeds and started gorging itself.

More than satisfied with this spectacularly close observation, we headed home. An exhausting eight-and-a-half hour day just to see a very rare lifebird and Manitoba first. I guess I've done crazier things. (We did spot another seventeen birds during the day, par for a winter's drive in Manitoba, but I didn't keep a daily trip list.)

Two weeks later, another Gray-crowned Rosy-Finch showed up a mere ten minutes from my house. AARRRGH! Why couldn't I have waited? I chased after it anyway. This one was a "coastal" variant: a Hepburn's or Gray-cheeked Rosy-Finch: *Leucosticte tephrocotis littoralis*. Similarly pushy at a feeder, it has more grey on the head, specifically on the "cheeks."

A couple of days later, a third Rosy-Finch showed up in the province, this one another "interior" bird. It was clear that something had forced these birds out of their native habitat. From fifteen appearances in Manitoba in 120 years to three sightings in one year—something's going on. In Northwestern Ontario, north of Lake Superior, several other Rosy-Finches were spotted that winter—a perfect eruption!

I didn't chase this third finch—or the ones in Ontario. I was happy with the two I'd gotten, one lifer and one possible future lifer—if the American Birding Association, the authority on naming and categorizing birds, someday decides to split the species in two.

I'm really looking forward to that. DNA tests by bird scientists have recently determined that some species are not that closely related; they are really two or three separate species. Expanded or altered lists are published almost every year. That's how you can add rare species to your life lists or provincial lists from the comfort of your own living room. It's far better than driving to the other side of the province and standing in the brutal cold.

Mississippi Kites
Alien Visitors

At 6:01 pm, a tradesman walked out of a huge, unfinished mansion being built on the ritzy, river side of Wellington Crescent. Five of us were standing in the median, regularly raising our binoculars, and sharing small talk. As he crossed the boulevard at the intersection of Montrose Street, toting a plastic lunch cooler and sweaty from a full day's work, he stopped to question us.

"What's goin' on?" he asked. "All day long, every time I looked out the windows, I've seen people standing out here with binoculars. Whattya lookin' for?"

The devil in me tempted me to say, mischievously, "Aliens!" But I bit my tongue.

"Mississippi Kites," I said. "Grey, hawk-like birds that shouldn't be anywhere near here. About the size of a crow."

Just then one of the other watchers yelled, "There it is!"

We all swung our binoculars up and caught a glimpse of a sleek, grey raptor south of Wellington and flying west. It kept disappearing and reappearing behind the elm and spruce trees, but its shape, colour, and flight behaviour were distinctive.

"Yes!" someone yelled, perhaps me. "That's it. That's the kite."

It was too soon gone. But we'd all seen enough to be enthused.

Even the tradesman saw it. He immediately thanked us and headed for his van. "Interesting hobby," he said—without a touch of irony or condescension.

Mississippi Kites, as the forename implies, shouldn't be in Manitoba. They're Dixie birds, usually confining themselves to the deep southern US. Finding one in Manitoba, where they've never been seen before, is cause for a celebration.

At first glance they can be mistaken for Peregrine Falcons, raptors that have nested successfully in downtown Winnipeg for the past thirty years. That's what Michael Loyd avid photographer and birder, assumed when he first saw a raptor on his daily jog through this neighbourhood. Kites are the same size and profile as Peregrines. But once he took photos, he knew he was onto something.

He reported his findings to the local Yahoo! Group called Manitobabirds. That was on Sunday evening, July 27. Long-time birder, and birding friend of mine, Andy Courcelles was at his computer when the message arrived. He dropped everything and rushed out to see if he could find the bird before dusk. He did. Back home, he quickly confirmed Mike's wonderful discovery.

The next morning, members of Winnipeg's birding community descended en masse on the Wellington/Montrose intersection. In mid-afternoon, John Weier, one of Manitoba's keenest birders, and others realized that not one but two kites were flying overhead at the same time. As the day wore on, more and more birders confirmed the news: there was a pair of kites in the area.

My sighting of one bird at 6:05 pm was satisfying enough that I could enter it into my life list and my provincial rare bird list. The first time I'd ever seen the bird, and of course, the first time I'd seen it in Manitoba. But I was not contented enough to leave the scene. Just "ticking" the bird, checking it off your list, was not enough. I like to observe the bird's behaviour, get the bird's markings and flight patterns firmly planted in my mind so that I can recognize it at a glance if or when I see it again. I stuck around to share the experience with the other birders. If there were two, I needed to see both birds.

As we waited, we all wondered how and why Mississippi Kites would venture so far from their usual haunts. It was as if Martians or other space aliens had shown up in Manitoba. The reason for their appearance is something we'll never really know. That's part of the thrill of their discovery. The mystery of it.

Then, as if by telepathy, a kite appeared magically to our west. It sailed slowly on the winds just above the treetops, directly overhead. It was so close we could see it catching dragonflies on the wing.

Kites do not have the direct, powerful, high-speed flight of Peregrines. They are graceful and almost gymnastic, with very maneuverable tails that allow them to soar and swoop and change direction suddenly. As if in response to our wishes, it adjusted its tail, banked upward into the sun, and showed the subtlety of its colours.

The kite's body and head were light grey; the under-wings were also grey but with some darker colour on the trailing part and near the tips; the upper wings had dull white patches; the tail was black. Everything showed up crystal clear in the sunlight. The bird was so close we could even see its red eyes. Red as small beacons. Then a second bird sailed into view behind it. "Oh, wow," someone said (not me), perhaps in imitation of the owner of a rare painting priced at fifty grand on the *Antiques Roadshow*. "Double wow!" In my binoculars I saw the first kite dip and catch a dragonfly on the wing. "Triple wow!"

It was the kind of exceptional viewing experience that every birder lusts after. I was totally chuffed, as the Brits say.

Whether they were intrepid explorers, blown here by a storm, or the victims of faulty, inbred GPS systems now became the question among us. That question was soon answered, or at least partially.

Not satisfied with just seeing the birds, members of the birding community set out to find a nest. It seemed like a long shot. That would mean that the birds had been here for at least several weeks without being noticed. However, there is a reason they are sometimes called the "stealth raptors," and why luck plays a part in all rare bird sightings.

By Thursday a nest was found. In it was a baby kite. The kites were a successful breeding pair. Since breeding pairs often return to successful nest-sites, and young birds can return to the place of their birth, we believed that this could be the start of something unique in all of Canada. Perhaps they wouldn't be such rare birds in the future.

Like savvy actors, the kites had appeared dramatically at just the right time. A Manitoba Breeding Bird Atlas, a heroic attempt to pinpoint the total number of all birds breeding throughout the province, was in the final weeks of a five-year investigation. The kites were the culminating discovery of the work of thousands of volunteers, work that had already changed the distribution maps of many other species. This would definitely be *the* highlight of the Manitoba Breeding Bird Atlas.

Unfortunuately, almost a month after its birth, the fledgling kite fell out of its nest. A group of concerned birders scooped it up and returned it to the nest. But the parents, likely first-year birds, were not prepared to take it back. They abandoned the nest. The baby kite, in surprisingly good health, was rescued and turned over to an avian rescue center. Sadly, it will never be able to be released into the wild again. It now serves as a demonstration bird, a kite teacher. While one adult kite was observed briefly the following year, the birding community will have to content itself with the demonstration kite, a captive and therefore un-list-able, but a beautiful bird to keep memories alive.

Northern Cardinal
Rare Bird, Alert

Before he moved back to southern Ontario to be closer to his family, George Holland patrolled the river's edge at Assiniboine Park like a scrupulous government accountant inspecting a billionaire's tax forms. Especially during spring migration (around tax time), he was meticulous about checking every bush and tree and leaf-littered hollow to see what new birds had arrived. Nothing went unseen or unheard.

When a rare bird showed up in the park—one that wouldn't normally be found in Manitoba—George would inform other interested birders of its whereabouts. He'd make the first call on the Rare Bird Alert phone chain. The phone chain of fifteen to twenty birders was the way bird news circulated before the internet. The bird discoverer would phone someone who would phone the next in line on the list who would phone someone else, etc., until the circuit was completed.

George would be at Assiniboine Park's eastern edge at dawn on virtually every non-stormy day in the month of May—the peak time of the northward migration season. I'd join him whenever I could since he was not only a great birder but a boon companion. Our morning greetings hardly ever varied. They were almost as ritualistic as a Trappist monk's Matins.

"Gene, good to see ya, me lad."

"Always good to see you, George."

"How the hell are ya?"

"If I felt any better, George, I'd have to be twins."

"The world ain't big enough for two of ya!"

If we were alone, he'd regale me with funny stories about his time in the military. And I'd try to match his stories with yarns about university life. He was a great tutor. I miss those days.

One May I was able to get to the park much more often than usual. That spring, with George's help, I saw almost every warbler and vireo and sparrow and flycatcher that a Manitoban could possibly see. Some of them were "lifers," first time sightings, like Canada Warblers with their brilliant yellow undersides and black necklaces and the well-named Black-throated Green Warblers. Others were more run-of-the-mill. Unremarkable vireos— Warbling, Red-eyed, and Blue-headed—told one from another mainly by their songs. Drab, grey flycatchers. And some brilliantly coloured warblers, usually seen in good numbers every spring.

But what stands out for me that spring was the arrival of a male Northern Cardinal. I'd seen them often as a kid, back east where they are common even in the winter. But they are rare enough in Manitoba that they need to be phoned around on the Rare Bird Alert. Cardinals have a distinctive, loud whistle—almost like a wolf-whistle. The first day we heard him, the bird was singing in full-throated, spring-time urgency. We heard him from maybe a quarter of a mile away and found him easily. He was at the top of a budding tree along the river, hundreds of miles north of his normal range. His red crest was cocked forward and his tail pointed down, perched there more vertically erect than a Mountie at attention. After a while, he moved across the river and then back into the park but across the meadow.

For weeks, he was somewhere in Assiniboine Park every day that I was there. You couldn't miss him calling insistently, hoping that a female cardinal would respond to his rapturous pleas. (Female cardinals, almost uniquely, can whistle like males.)

George and I often wondered outloud about the bird. What ill-wind or foolish sense of adventure brought him here? What landmarks had he overflown? Was he lonely, bewildered, frustrated? It's difficult to keep from anthropomorphizing birds, especially if, like George and I, you are a migrant like him.

We also worried about this rare bird, alert to the empty silences between his calls but inattentive to the potential dangers of this new place.

The Cooper's Hawks that have nested in the park south of the pedestrian bridge for years must have taken notice of his self-advertising. Their diet includes songbirds of all types, especially noisy, unwary ones.

One foggy morning, after two weeks or so, George and I got to the park and immediately noticed the absence of the cardinal's piercing whistle. Had he simply flown on—who knows where—when he'd gotten no response to his mating calls? Or had one of the hungry, unsympathetic Cooper's Hawks feasted on his flesh? (We never did find a pile of fire engine red feathers that would have signaled he'd been caught and devoured.) Can birds die of unrealized expectations or broken hearts?

The park was emptier than usual that morning. Migration season was coming to an end. The missing cardinal's whistle made it seem far too quiet. I told George that this was perhaps the melancholy feeling we'd have every migrating season if Rachel Carson's predictions in *Silent Spring* came true. Carson noted the devastating effects of DDT on bird populations and predicted that there'd be fewer and fewer birds returning each spring to help us feel a sense of vitality and renewal. DDT was outlawed, but we still live in an over-chemicalized world and habitat destruction continues unabated. Even optimists can sense disappointment on the horizon.

Indigo Bunting or Lazuli
What the Heck Is It?

[What follows is an approximation. All profanity has been excised or bowdlerized; it is now suitable for all ages—including my grandsons.]

In order to get better, seasoned birders will tell you that you must go birding often and on your own if necessary. That's a given! Birding is no different than any other pursuit. To be proficient you've got to put in the hours—according to some, 10,000 hours.

So, one fine May day, you decide to go out birding on your own. You've got your bird book and don't think twice about bringing along a smartphone; you don't own one. You don't even carry your picture-taking dumb-phone or your camera or your iPad. You're all by your lonesome, ill-equipped, along a bark-covered path among the trees in St. Vital Park when you catch a glimpse of something that you're not quite sure of. You look again. It's gone.

You scratch your head. Was that what you think it was? A Bluebird? What is a Bluebird doing here in this habitat? Bluebirds prefer open terrain where they can sit on hydrolines and fences and catch bugs. You don't think a Bluebird has ever been here before. Something ain't right. Gull dang it!

It's a beautiful spring day. You soldier on, half-hoping you'll catch sight of the bird again, half-hoping you won't. Well, I'll be horn-grebed! you say to yourself. There it is again! Odd song for a Bluebird. More like an Indigo Bunting's. Can't be an Indigo Bunting; an Indigo is all blue.

Le'me check my battered but trustworthy bird book (*National*

Geographic Field Guide to the Birds of North America). Hmmm. Blue back, white belly, and pinkish breast. Not a Blue Grosbeak, an exotic from the southwest. Could it possibly be a Lazuli Bunting? If that's what it is, and you're not totally sure, you'll have to let other birders know. That's a rare bird around here. Better get a good, long look.

You raise your binoculars, and the gad-walloped bird has disappeared again. Dog-nab it! Back to the book. You go through it page by page, hoping to eliminate everything it can't be. Hmmm. Maybe it is a Lazuli Bunting. Then again, maybe not. It's not quite an exact replica of the book's Lazuli. Not to worry. Drawings in bird guides are generalities. Individual anomalies happen.

But it's just gotta be a Lazuli Bunting. What else could it be? An oddball Indigo Bunting with a rouge-stained breast? Not really.

What if it's not a Lazuli? Better double-check again. Still not sure. Better triple- or quadruple-check. Hoar frost on a damp pippit! You wish you'd brought something to get a photo of the bird!

You remember the time you thought you saw a Northern Mockingbird. It was late winter, the ground still covered with snow. The sun shining brightly. You were without your binoculars or bird book. The bird was high in a tree, flitting around. You had to squint to see it.

A slender grey bird with a longish tail, robin-sized, white underneath with wing bars. It's a, um, a Northern Mockingbird. Finally! You'd been chasing this bird for years.

You're so pumped, you throw all caution to the wind and rush home to notify other birders. They'll certainly want to see it if it's absent from their Manitoba lists. Northern Mockingbirds are notoriously tough to see in Manitoba.

Two hours later you get a phone call. That wasn't a Northern Mockingbird; it was a Townsend's Solitaire. You never even thought of that possibility. It too is a somewhat rare bird here. You've seen it a couple of times. It's long and slender too, with wing patches. A duller grey, this bird looked white underneath like a mockingbird because of the reflection off the snow.

You remember the embarrassment of that misidentification. But you also remember the elation of correctly identifying a rare Gull-billed Tern in Bermuda. You found it on an inland pond in the north of the island.

You checked and double-checked. Tern-like in size and colour. Short, thick bill. Long, black legs. You fretted and cursed. Then you phoned the rare bird hotline and reported it. Hours later, your sighting was confirmed. First sighting of the bird in a long time. You cracked it. Fantastic! Fabulous feeling! A move up to the A-listers.

Now, the possible Lazuli Bunting is another story. Conflicted, you head home, get on the internet, check your manitobabirds emails, and discover that someone else has already seen it and put out a notice. Oh, well. You won't get credit for discovering it (not that this is tallied in St. Peter's book of good deeds and will get you a heavenly seat next to St. Francis of Assisi!). But at least you were correct in your identification.

Other members of the Winnipeg birding community flock to the Lazuli location. They see it and grumble. Disputes arise. After several days and some good, clear photos, it's decided that the bird is in fact a hybrid: a Lazuli Bunting crossed with an Indigo Bunting. No wonder you had so much trouble identifying the bird!

Advice-givers tell you that you must go birding on your own in order to get better. That's a given! But sometimes when you're birding alone, you find yourself wishing that somebody, anybody, was right next to you to help you confirm that what you think you're seeing is actually what's there.

A Greylag
and Other Wild Goose Chases

If you are at all interested in finding rare birds, you know that luck is often a factor in spotting them. For birds, the sky is literally the limit. They can flit into an area and skip out in seconds. You're driving along a country road and suddenly a big, grey bird flashes past. You slam on the brakes, grab your binocs, and get a good look just before it disappears over the trees. A Gyrfalcon, the largest of the falcons and the toughest to find. Great!

For strays or vagrants—birds not native to a particular environment—a rare sighting depends even more on luck. Bird-luck.

Mockingbirds are especially undependable. Aptly named, they seem to mock my every attempt to find them, even when I get to the place where they've been spotted only minutes before. It took me years—and more than a dozen false alarms—before I added them to my Manitoba list.

A Scissor-tailed Flycatcher spotted by others in Portage la Prairie many years ago almost drove me around the bend. On four different occasions, I drove out to Portage at about the speed of Vin Diesel in *The Fast and the Furious* movies. Four wild goose chases. More than twenty other birding friends were lucky enough to see it—many of them on their first try, no less. I never saw it. Still haven't, even though I recently chased after one east of Winnipeg. The birding gods were against me.

Likewise, the Black-throated Sparrow that showed up in a farmyard just off Highway 75 in St. Jean Baptiste a few years back. It was reported by the farm-owners on a Friday night. I couldn't get there on Saturday when this adventurer from the southwest USA seemed to bask in the constant attention of dozens of excited birders. By the time my friend John and I got there early Sunday morning, it was not to be found. We scoured the trees and bushes in the area and kept a watchful eye on the places it frequented the day before. No luck. Eight or ten more birders showed up. No help from them either, except that we were all separately trying to will the bird to return.

After three hours of futile waiting, I knew I had to get back to Winnipeg. But here's where birding superstition sets in: we were all reluctant to go, all waiting for someone else to leave first. It was a game of birding chicken. The fear is: as soon as the first impatient birder leaves, the bird will show up. John and I waited past the point of patience. But we wouldn't give up. Finally, someone else had had enough and decided to leave. We all tensed and looked around with extra special care. The bird was still a no-show. Then another couple left. And then we did. About a dozen others had followed us to the St. Jean Baptiste farm that day. As a friend of mine says, we were all bad-lucky.

As frustrating as those non-encounters were, they don't match the frustration of finding a dead rare bird. John once found a freshly killed Barn Owl west of Winnipeg; there are very few records of live ones here. An ex-Barn Owl is uncountable. A newly dead Black-legged Kittiwake found, I believe, in the parking lot at Stony Mountain Institution, is a local legend. Ex-kittiwakes are also uncountable, even still-warm ones. The reasoning: maybe someone kidnapped the kittiwake, drove to Stony Mountain, got tired of the bird, strangled it, and left it in the parking lot. Far-fetched, but enough to rule it out as a live sighting. Birders are as honest and honourable as nuns. Far better than some amateur golfers—five shots to the green, three putts = six on the scorecard!

Finding a living rare bird and having it declared un-countable is even more frustrating. A Greylag once led me on a real wild goose chase. Well, maybe not wild. And that was the problem.

Manitoba is not a goose-free zone. It's on a major north-south migration super highway. Upwards of 200,000 geese fly in and out every spring and fall. To be at Oak Hammock Marsh when wave after wave of them wing in and then wiffle down onto the open water is a sight to behold.

Magnificent! Stirring! (To be in St. Vital Park or on a provincial golf course after the geese use them as biffies is less inspiring.)

Most of the geese are Snows and Canadas, with regular sightings of Ross's and Greater White-fronts, and, much more rarely, Brants. And never, ever Greylag Geese.

So, when a notice was posted of a Greylag Goose at a retention pond in an east Winnipeg industrial park, I was there in a flash.

The Greylag is native to Europe and Asia. Although other Eurasian Geese are slowly making their way to North America, only one wild (and banded) Greylag has ever been officially accepted as a trans-Atlantic migrant. All the other Greylags have been classified as released or escaped domestic geese or hybrids. They're good-eatin' and therefore common farmyard geese, as I found out later.

Rudolf Koes, originally from Greylag country and now one of the best birders in Canada, had a close look at this bird. "It is too large for a pure Greylag," he declared. "The neck is too thick, the bill too high, and it has the droopy fold of skin and feathers between the legs which is seen in domestic birds." In other words, it was a domestic bird, an escapee, probably a hybrid; ergo, it was ineligible for lists.

Well, maybe for primary, official lists. But I keep a supplementary list, begun when an escaped Chukar, probably raised at a nearby game-bird farm, hung around the University of Manitoba campus fourteen years ago. (I checked my list.) I saw it often, pointing out, mischievously, to whomever was nearby, "This is a phantom bird; it can't be counted. It doesn't really exist."

Besides, I'm actually less interested in the "ticking" than in the sightings of rare birds, no matter what their provenance.

Birding is about wonderment. With the Greylag, I keep wondering: where did it come from? How did it get here? Where did it go? What tempter or temptress lured it from its comfy but doomed barnyard existence? Did it suddenly sing, like Daffy Duck, "I mutht go where the wild goothe goeth?" How did it manage to keep up with the Canada Geese vee-squad it joined up with? Will it find another farm far south of here in the Canadas' wintering grounds and settle there for the year-round warmth? Or will it bond with the Canadas and fly back north in the spring? I'll probably never know.

Burrowing Owls
A Trip to FortWhyte Alive

One cold winter when my older grandson, Torsten, was three, he came to visit me here in Winnipeg from his home in Switzerland. Nyon, the town where he lives in Switzerland, is pretty mild in the winter. Winnipeg winters ain't mild! The Swiss Alps and the Jura get piles of snow but Nyon is on Lake Leman (aka Lake Geneva); snow there usually lasts a day or two before it melts away. Torsten barely understands what a real winter is all about.

I took him to the required Winnipeg sight-seeing spots: the Children's Museum, the Manitoba Museum, Manitoba Theatre for Young People, Tim Horton's (they still had the apostrophe then), and, of course, the zoo. It was minus twenty-something, but at the zoo you can warm up in the inside exhibits and race through the frigid air between them, glancing quickly at whatever hardy animals are forced to stay outside. We stayed longest at the outside bird enclosures. Raptors and owls—big birds, the kinds that kids can see and marvel at even with frost on their eyelids.

We spent the longest time, maybe thirty-one seconds, at the "Snow" Owl (his term) cage. He was fascinated by their bright yellow eyes and their large, dangerous talons. I pointed out the difference between the males and females—males almost entirely white, females with black streaks. Then we raced back inside to warm up.

As the circulation slowly returned to our feet, I told him more about the "Snow" Owls. They eat arctic rodents called lemmings and when there aren't enough lemmings to go around, they migrate south to Manitoba. I think I may have told him about the owls in the *Harry Potter* books and movies. (Confession: I've only read one of the books and sat through only one movie.) Six years later, my grandson has now seen all of the *Harry Potter* movies and is slowly making his way through JK Rowling's books. So he's hooked on owls (his favourite one is, I think, Harry's "Snow" Owl, Hedwig), though he's probably forgotten I showed him his first live one.

When we left, it occurred to me that I was coddling the kid. So the next day I bundled him into every layer of winter clothing I could find, including scarf, toque, and ski-mask, and we set out for FortWhyte Alive, a former quarry which is now a nature reserve in west Winnipeg.

Our first stop at FortWhyte was the buffalo pasture. I know, I know, there are no "buffaloes" in North America. They are *bison*. But like many three-year-olds, my grandson had trouble with his r's and l's. I just loved to hear him say buffayoes!

This 500-acre buffayo enclosure is a far cry from the crummy zoos of my childhood. Durand Eastman Park in Rochester, New York had a "zoo" but it was really an animal jail. It was in a deep gully about forty by twenty yards with a high fence that kept a couple of elk, a handful of skinny deer, and one miserable, shaggy, old bison. He was the first live one I ever saw—the first one that was not on the back of a US nickel. If you stomped your feet and uttered a few deep woofs, that testy, old bison would charge the rickety fence. We would wait until some unsuspecting zoo visitors (usually young women) approached the fence, then stomp and woof. The bull would charge, and we'd see how high-pitched their screams would get and how fast they could run. Ah, you may think, a sad case of runaway teenage hormones! But most of the crew were older than forty. Testosterone freaks!

It's said that there were once up to 75 million plains bison in North America. By the middle of the nineteenth century, only about half of them remained. Still, there were enough that when Sitting Bull left Canada to surrender to the US army in 1881, he rode through a single, continuous herd for nine straight days.

Millions of bison, the ninth largest land animal in the world, used to graze the prairies of Manitoba. But size and numbers could not save them from people bent on simple slaughter. In 1895, Ernest Thomson Seton, the great Manitoba naturalist, could count only 800 bison in the province. Shortly thereafter, their numbers dwindled to 500 on the entire continent.

Now, there are more than twice that number in our province (some of them actually wild) and over half a million in North America. But their numbers owe more to bison ranching than to conservation. Of course, I didn't mention any of this to my grandson. Well, I did mention that we were lucky to see them because long ago people slaughtered millions and millions of them and they became so rare they almost became extinct. When he asked me what extinct meant, I explained and then cut my lecture short. I have to constantly resist the urge to overpower him with facts, to blurt out everything I know or almost know in one grandfatherly gush. I just let him take it all in. Wonder at it and maybe worry.

Bison are truly impressive beasts. When my grandson and I visited, it was a blustery cold day with almost a foot of snow on the ground. Great snorts of breath blasted from their nostrils, and they rooted for grass by shagging away the snow with their great triangular heads. I could see why their heads hang lower than almost any other animal. They don't have to bend down to eat, having evolved to graze efficiently on prairie grasses. Too bad there's so little left.

At FortWhyte Alive, I got my grandson to stomp his little feet and woof, as I did as a skinny, teenaged, road-gang member back in Rochester. But these particular buffayoes paid no attention to us.

Then we raced inside to see a stuffed buffayo up close (the ones outside were fifty metres away). We stomped our feet at it too, but it didn't move a muscle either. Then we strolled back into the Interpretive Centre to look at all the taxidermied birds and beasts on display.

Torsten was most impressed, and a bit scared, by the stuffed polar bear, the cougar, the wolf and the black bear. I had to reassure him that he was quite safe because none of them had eaten the stuffed tom turkey; they didn't seem interested in a potential meal that would have been much tastier than him. I quickly steered him to the walls of mounted birds. Lots of owls, big and small, from a Screech Owl and a Saw-whet Owl to a Great Grey and a Snowy. I read the plaques to identify them, but that's all. No lessons in distinguishing one from another. Although they look faded and weather-beaten, dead birds like this are better educators than photos, drawings, and even movies. A kid gets a better idea of size and dimensions. He can understand feathers and fur by touching them gently (when no one's looking).

From the stuffed owls we made a bee-line, or an owl-line, for the newly opened Burrowing Owl reclamation space. The scurrying prairie dogs quickly captured his attention. Who isn't amused by these funny little creatures? It took a while and some hints from me for Torsten to discover the owls. One was standing in a hole. A burrow, I pointed out, like a tunnel; he'd never heard the word. That's where they live, underground. Then the owl seemed to notice us. It tilted its head sideways and gave that little shimmy-shake that Burrowing Owls do to get a three-dimensional view. This proved more amusing than the prairie dogs to Torsten.

We talked more about owls on the way home. I told him that I once could see Burrowing Owls just outside Winnipeg. Now there are hardly any in Manitoba. They're so rare that their whereabouts are a closely guarded secret. People do that, sometimes unwittingly, to animals like the bison and the Burrowing Owl: take them right to the edge of extinction. Maybe FortWhyte will raise enough Burrowing Owls to re-stock the province. Maybe when he's my age, he can just drive out to LaSalle as I did and see them in the wild.

I've since bought Torsten some binoculars and a bird book, but I'm not trying to make him a birder or an ornithologist. I'd just like it if he comes to appreciate the outdoors and not get stuck gaping at a cell phone or a laptop all day long. Angry Birds may be a captivating video game, but it's nothing compared to seeing live birds and animals. I hope he resists the urge to become a slave to technology and is more comfortable in nature, alert to its liveliness, power, and beauty.

Apapanes
and Other Hawaiian Birds

Hawaii is not the place to go if you're intent on adding to your life-bird list. There just aren't that many unique native birds left on the islands.

Since "civilization" reached Hawaii about 200 years ago, over thirty native birds have gone extinct. It has the worst record for extirpation of any state. Beyond the effects of colonization, recent evidence seems to suggest that more species were killed off by the original islanders than was originally suspected, since bird plumage played a huge role in their costumes and decoration. Additionally, avian tuberculosis devastated a lot of the Hawaiian native birds, and since then, well-intentioned people from various continents who have brought along their caged or neighbourhood birds and then set them free to displace native birds have caused many of the problems. Tourism and rampant development also hasn't helped much.

When a friend and I were in Maui in January, 2013, I did see about three dozen species of birds. But most of them I had seen or could have seen elsewhere: cardinals, manakins, white-eyes, the usual introduced species, some common shorebirds and water birds from the Americas, and others. There was even a colony of Peach-faced Lovebirds thriving in south Kihei—so new to Maui that they aren't yet mentioned in any of the bird guides for the island.

I take delight in finding and identifying all kinds of birds, but there's something disappointing in seeing non-tropical birds on tropical islands.

Especially if they are contributing to the demise of the native birds, the endemics—rare birds you can't see anywhere else. Invasive species are often bullies; they take over the habitats and food sources of endemics.

One of the last places to see Maui endemics is in Hosmer's Grove, a canyon near the top of the extinct volcano Haleakala on the east side of the island. Haleakala is the mountain that tourists visit at dawn to watch the sun rise over the water. We drove through the clouds to get to Hosmer's Grove. The air was crisp and fresh with the smell of flower blossoms on the trees.

In two separate visits, I managed to get long, satisfying views of such rare native species as the Apapane (a brilliant red honeycreeper), Amakihi (a yellow-green honeycreeper), Alauahio (similar enough to the Amakihi to make identification a challenge), and I'iwi (like the Apapane but with black wings and a huge, curved bill). They're all bright, active, wonderful bird finds. For me, part of the pleasure of seeing them is the challenge of learning to pronounce and then savour their musical, Hawaiian names.

But I missed the Kiwikiu (Maui Parrotbill) and Akohekohe (Crested Honeycreeper), two high-priority target-birds. A huge disappointment. They are becoming increasingly rare, rapidly disappearing on the island and struggling to survive.

Nearby I found several rare NeNe (Hawaiian Geese) and in the shallows at the Kealia Pond National Wildlife Refuge I easily spotted Alae Kea (Hawaiian Coots), Koloa Maoli (Hawaiian Ducks), and many Ae'o (Hawaiian Stilts). They may sound exotic, but they look pretty much like their North American counterparts, so they're not all that special. In fact, the Hawaiian Ducks were re-introduced to Maui after hybridizing with some not-so-very-rare-at-all Mallards.

Not every trip I take is devoted exclusively to birding. In many cases, birding takes up only a small portion of my time. I went to Maui for the whale-watching, the seafood and fresh fruit, the beaches, and the warmth. Especially the warmth! It would have been great had I been able to get good, long looks at all the bird species I targeted, though. I guess I'll have to go back and look a bit harder. In the warmth. Damn!

Andean Cock of the Rock
The Bird Gods Smile on Us

Sometimes I feel as though I've been given a thousand blessings from the elusive and unpredictable gods of birding.

Up at 3:00 am after maybe four hours of fitful sleep. Eat breakfast from a bag on a bouncy van ride through total darkness to a parking area somewhere in the Andes, east of Quito, Ecuador. Walk in dismal blackness up and down bumpy trails, slippery with mud and tree roots. My head is a blizzard of pain. My arthritic knees and hips throb and ache. Why on God's green earth (now black and indecipherable) am I doing this?!

Three of us were hoping to find the elusive Andean Cock of the Rock deep down in the western shadow of the Andes at the Paz de las Aves Bird Refuge. It was supposed to be at its lek—a place where male birds strut and battle for the attention of observant females. We had to be near the lek before dawn so as not to spook the bird or birds. If we stumbled noisily down the steep trail, chances were, it would not make an appearance. Our special guide, Angel Paz, owner of the property, led us downward in the pitch blackness with the aid of a thin pencil of light. Even if we did get to the lek on time, the bird might not show up. After a twenty- to thirty-minute descent, Angel unexpectedly turned to us and held up his hand. My eyes had adjusted, but it was still so dark that I bumped into him. We stood stock still as he walked farther down to check on the arrival of the birds. When he returned, he led us to our spotting site and motioned for us to be quiet. Shifting carefully and uncomfortably from foot to foot, we waited an agonizing eternity. We were so far down the ravine that glimmers of light came to the sky well before anything reached where we were.

Suddenly, from the depths of the thick darkness of the ravine, I saw a pinpoint of flame red, almost like the flash of a Chevy tail light at the far end of a long tunnel. As the red light hopped and flitted from branch to branch and drew closer, we could see that it was the bird we were after: a magnificent male Andean Cock of the Rock. It seemed like an emissary from some fiery place deep inside the bowels of the earth. An ambulatory eternal flame.

Larger than a Blue Jay, the Cock of the Rock has brilliant scarlet or orange plumage, black and grey wings, a black tail, and a large disk-like crest. From the side, the crest makes it look like it's got a giant red knob, almost as big as its head, extending from the tip of its beak to the middle of its head. It's truly bizarre.

As we watched, transfixed, a second bird appeared out of the darkness and then a third. Usually shy, inconspicuous, and seen only briefly, the three males began doing what male birds do at a lek: performing an odd mating ritual to attract nearby breeding females. They displayed their colourful red plumage by flapping their wings, bobbing, hopping, shimmying, and jumping up and down from branch to branch while uttering a variety of low, guttural calls. If there were females around, we couldn't see them; they are a drab, chestnut brown and were perhaps watching at a safe, hidden distance lest a bunga bunga party break out.

I don't know how long the performances lasted. Time seemed to be irrelevant in this low, dark place. Gradually the three birds lost interest in their own croaking (which would have been hilarious if the birds were not so strikingly coloured). Then they flitted off into the darkness they'd emerged from. Despite the rising sun behind the mountains, the darkness was still almost total when they finally disappeared.

There was a moment of deflation while we returned to the normal world. Then exhilaration. Wow! We had just seen one of the great birds of the world and been privy to one of the most remarkable spectacles in nature. That's why we'd put up with all the aches and pains to get here. The outside world with all its hassles and personal grief had evaporated. The great novelist Vladimir Nabokov once wrote, somewhere, about finding

finding luminosity in a world that has somehow ceased to be a source of delight. That's what finding a glorious, rare bird like the Andean Cock of the Rock can do.

Antpittas
The Bird Gods Spurn Us

Then again, I often feel that I've been dealt a thousand curses by the abusive and unreliable gods of birding.

The darkened, leaf-littered floors of the tropical forests of Ecuador are home to billions of ants. These ants attract all kinds of ant-following birds: antbirds, antwrens, antshrikes, ant-tanagers, ant-thrushes, antvireos, and, the funniest looking of them all, the antpittas—also the ones with the oddest name. They are mostly brown, inconspicuous birds of the forest floor, feeding not so much on ants but the other insects that ants (especially army ants) scare up. Antbirds are usually difficult or virtually impossible to see, especially the antpittas.

On the very same day that we were fortunate enough to see the Cocks of the Rock, we went looking for other rarities. Paz de las Aves in the high Andes, where we found the Cocks of the Rock, is also known for attracting antpittas. The Paz family, especially brothers Angel and Rodrigo, first learned that antpittas could be lured out of hiding by offering them meal-worms. The brothers have even learned to mimic the antpitta's call to signal that the mealworms have been set out. Paz's pittas, sort of like Pavlov's dogs.

Our new target bird is a Giant Antpitta. We are guided quietly to a secluded place where this bird feeds. It's not there yet. We trudge back up the steep path, still in darkness, and wait for a signal from Angel. When it comes, we clamber quietly down to the viewing spot. Still no bird. We head back up the trail and wait. We feel like mute versions of Vladimir and Estragon in *Waiting for Godot*.

Vladimir and Estragon did not have to deal with weather. We do. Ecuador has two seasons: wet and dry. Luckily, we were in the Andes in the dry season. But as any Ecuadorian will tell you, "In the dry season it rains every day; in the wet season it rains all day." We get a little wet—not uncomfortably soaked, just annoyingly dampened.

As we wait, we check our bird books. The Giant Antpitta is a strange creature. About the size of a small crow, at first glance it looks like a large thrush that's had its tail chopped off and is standing at attention. Its plumage is mostly deep rufous-brown except for a grey streak running from the top of its head and down its neck. The throat and breast feathers are orange with black edges, resulting in a dark barring. The legs are half as long as the body; it stands on them as erect as Abe Lincoln.

Our overall tour guide, has never seen this particular kind of antpitta or many other antbirds; they were notoriously difficult to see until the Paz brothers developed their antpitta feeding strategy. So we traipse up and down the trail several more times—far too many—before Angel Paz declares that the Giant Antpitta must be on its nest. It will not be lured away by mere mealworms. Our guide is hugely disappointed; we are sad but relieved. Yes, we miss an important target-bird, but we've no more mountainside hiking to endure. A near relative, the extraordinarily rare and vulnerable Mustached Antpitta, also fails to put in an appearance. In the book, it looks like a large robin with a white malar stripe (mustache) and no tail. We do hear it off in the undergrowth and we consider that a bonus since it's almost never seen. We can enter the bird onto our lists as "heard-only", but this is a bit disappointing since some listing sticklers consider this "non-sighting" as un-list-able.

The day quickly turns into an extended quest for antpittas. Antpitta. Antpitta. Antpitta. Midway through the day, all I can think of is The Pita Pit, a restaurant where you can get wraps full of fresh veggies and meat. An Ant Pita. A wrap crawling with ants. Luis Buñuel's film *Un Chien Andalou,* where ants seem to crawl out of a wound in the palm of a hand, comes to mind. Aaarrgh!

Carted to another mealworm site, we finally get to see one—the tiny Ochre-breasted Antpitta, like a pint-sized thrush without a tail. The Paz brothers have taken to naming their antpittas; this one is called, for reasons unknown, Shakira. Later we come upon a mealworm-eating Ocelated

Antpitta (named Thomas), plus a near relative, the Ocelated Tapacula, another ant-swarm chaser, and a Yellow-breasted Antpitta (Willie, by name). They're all good "gets," birds that would have been impossible to see five or ten years ago, but they're hardly the kind to get your pulse racing like the magical Cock of the Rock. Or the Andean Condor, which we missed because our guide seemed more interested in seeing the rarities that he hadn't seen before rather than what we'd hoped to see.

Sometimes birding is simply an exercise in avian frustration.

Forty-spotted Pardalotes
Rare Australian Endemic

Endemics are birds found only in one place. Though they might be fairly common where they are, they are impossible to find anywhere else in the world. That gives them a special kind of rarity. If you're in a place where there are endemics and you don't find them, especially a place you'll likely never return to, you are doubly regretful. You try not to mention to your birding friends that you've been to that certain spot because you know that the first thing they'll ask you is: have you seen the special endemic found there? Then you just pass it off as bad-lucky.

The Atherton Tableland in Queensland, Australia is home to a tiny skulker called the Atherton Scrubwren. My wife and I spent a rainy afternoon trying to spot this plain, tawny-coloured little bird on the forest floor of a very small area. They were supposed to be there and only there; they weren't. All we got was wet. But we did find a small, clear, shallow river where eight duck-billed platypuses (platypi?) swam about. We wouldn't have found these odd creatures (like a genetic experiment gone wrong—matching duck, muskrat, and beaver DNA) had we not been searching for the nondescript scrubwren.

After Queensland, we flew to Tasmania, the heart-shaped island off the southeast coast of Australia. As soon as we got there, I started hunting for the island's twelve endemics. I was almost as anxious to find the island's endemic subspecies—four birds that have diverged from their mainland counterparts after time in isolation and now differ in certain physical features. Some day they might be split off into a separate species, so they're well worth hunting down. Who knows? I might get to add a bird or two to my lists without having to fly back to Taz.

It wasn't difficult to find a Tasmanian Wedge-tailed Eagle in the skies above Mount Wellington, the towering monolith overlooking the neat Victorian city of Hobart. Likewise, the Clinking Currawong (aren't Aussie names great?!), a variant on the Grey Currawong, was easy to spot on Wellington's trails. For the life of me, I couldn't see the differentiating features of these subspecies from the mainland's species. Since Wellington's trails were easily accessible to our nearby lodging, I tramped them regularly, picking up three endemics, the Tasmanian Thornbill, the Yellow Wattlebird, and the Yellow-throated Honeyeater, without much difficulty. On the beaches nearby, it was even easier spotting the Tasmanian Native Hen, a large gallinule that's unable to fly but can run as fast as a halfback. For the others, I knew I was going to need help.

Near the end of our stay, we booked a weekend at the Inala cottage on Bruny Island. Dr. Tonia Cochran promises that you can find all twelve endemics on her property or nearby. We figured it was worth the price—until we got there.

On the long drive from Hobart to Inala, we found two previously unseen endemics on our own: Green Rosellas, yellow-bodied parrots with blue cheeks and broad tails, and Dusky Robins, more like European robins than American and called "thickheads" because they look and act like colourful flycatchers (not because they are as dense as some reality TV stars). We also saw Pink and Flame Robins, two of the more colourful thickheads, their names describing their breast colours.

The most amusing pre-Inala sightings occurred along the isthmus connecting North and South Bruny Islands. On the sand dunes here are the nests of Short-billed Shearwaters, also known as Muttonbirds. They are graceful in the air above the waves, but when they land at dusk and after, they are as clumsy as flying sheep would be. They fly in, full-throttle, bang into the sand hills, and then waddle groggily to their burrows. Archie Bunker could easily classify them with his son-in-law: muttonheads.

In the evening when we arrived at Inala, I was easily able to find and identify the most sought-after bird in Tasmania—the Forty-spotted Pardalote. It's one of the smallest and rarest birds in Australia, classified endangered. A light olive green bird, it has black wings with distinctive white spots. To be honest, it was a disappointment. The Striated and the Spotted Pardalotes that hang out with the Forty-spotteds are more colourful and the Spotted ones seem to have more spots. Fifty? Sixty? I couldn't count the white dots on either of the small, jittery, treetop birds. I'll have to take the taxonomists' word and simply delight in savouring the tongue-twister name. Say it ten times: Forty-spotted Pardalotes, Forty-spotted Pardalotes....

That left four endemics for the guided birdwalk the next morning. It looked easy-peasy until we awoke to rain. Rain so torrential that it would scare Noah. Rain pouring from low, cement-grey clouds as if from giant waves. Then drizzly, annoying rain. Followed by steady and dispiriting rain. Then a downpour. What bird would possibly show its feathery, beaky face in this weather? None. It looked like we'd spent our money in vain. But Tonia sensed my frustration.

Halfway through the morning, after creeping along in her pickup and looking dejectedly out of steamy windows, Tonia accelerated up and around the twisty roads, heading towards the spot where Captain Cook landed. As we crested a hill, she slowed. I thought I saw a ghost. A pure white apparition or a strange animal of some sort at the far edge of a meadow. It kept bending over and rising up like a furry, white oil derrick.

It took me a full minute to figure out what it was. Tonia smiled.

"Is that what I think it is? An albino kangaroo?"

"Nope. It's a Bennett's wallaby." A smaller, cuddlier relative of kangaroos.

This one was almost pure white. Almost, except for a patch of brown around the mouth and nose. When it stood up, I put my binocs on it, and laughed. The wallaby was eating the leaves of a burdock bush, and the burrs were sticking to its face. It had an exaggerated mustache, almost like a Groucho Marx mustache. I laughed harder than I probably should have.

Before my time with Tonia was up, we'd seen three more albinos. Albinism is the result of isolation and inbreeding. Bruny Island is small and isolated enough to produce handfuls of albino Bennett's wallabies. When the rain finally subsided enough to draw the birds out, just before my time was up, we also scored my final four Tasmanian endemics: a

Black Currawong, a Black-headed and a Strong-billed Honeyeater, and a Tasmanian Scrubwren (aka Scrub-Tit). Whew! I got them all. Plus more than a dozen new species enjoying the post-rain sunshine as we drove slowly back to Hobart.

Birding does have its non-avian compensations. Although I had vigorously cursed the birding gods in the rain, I thanked them graciously for a very productive weekend. They had blessed me with all the Tasmanian endemics, and gifted me with the strange and amusing platypuses and the otherworldly wallabies. Birding expeditions have given me a lot more than just fabulous, rare birds.

The Resplendent Quetzal
My Favourite Bird

When people find out that I'm a birder, they invariably ask me what my favourite bird is. As a response, I'd sometimes suggest, impertinently, asking a doctor what his favourite body part is or a lawyer what his favourite law is. But I'm usually a genial conversationalist.

I understand the awkwardness and curiosity behind the question. For forty years I was a film prof, and people always asked me at some point what my favourite movie was. It's a natural way to start or prolong a party conversation. The trouble is, my answers usually vary. Favourite movie? *Dr. Strangelove, City Lights, Casablanca, Blade Runner, Wings of Desire, Jules and Jim*, etc., etc. Favourite bird? Frilled Coquette, Bare-faced Go-Away-Bird, Hoopoe, Blue Pitta, Hyacinth Macaw, Cock of the Rock, Great Grey Owl, etc., etc. (Google these to see why.) There are so many to choose from!

If cornered, if I really think about it, the answer always comes back to the Resplendent Quetzal, a bird that truly deserves its unique, descriptive adjective. It is one of the few birds that I can think of that should be called "resplendent." Definition: shining brilliantly, lustrous, glowing with blazing splendor.

It's a bird of contradictions, a bird that could have been designed by a Milanese haute couturier. The male seems to want to camouflage itself and show off at the same time. It has a luminous, neon-green head, as well as breast, wings, back, and top-side of the tail—the green like a lush, perfectly watered, fertilized, and brightly sunlit lawn. The green wings are scalloped in an artistic pattern and the head has a spiky, punk-style crest. But the underpart of the body is shiny, blood red and the underside of the tail is bright white. The crowning touch, at least in the male during breeding season, is a pair of metre-long, green tail feathers twice the length of its body. Flamboyance, thy name is quetzal.

Resplendent Quetzals are the perfect rare bird. As distinctive as they are, they are not plentiful and not easy to find. They sit dead still and silent for long periods of time in the darkly forested mountains of southern Mexico, Costa Rica, and Panama. You can pass right underneath them and miss them if you're not alert. Usually, you have to hear their deep and simple song to find them. Because they're so imperturbably stationary, they're easy to examine, once found. Sitting still, they look like they've been placed on a branch by a taxidermist. Or like they're posing in all their finery for a fashion magazine photographer.

It's always exciting to see a rare bird in the flesh, or, should I say, in the feathers. The bird is something you've seen in bird books in two-dimensions as a photo or a hand-drawn and coloured depiction, in some cases (*Peterson Field Guides*) with arrows pointing at its distinguishing features. Suddenly it's right in front of you, or through your binoculars, close enough, experienced in the now, as real as could be. Alive and in three quivering (or, in the case of quetzals, static) dimensions!

Finding a quetzal can be disconcerting as well. There's something eerie in its majestic stillness. Until it moves, even slightly. Then it can snap you back into reality—like a photo suddenly coming to life or a busker, posing convincingly as a statue, involuntarily sneezing.

Quetzals were considered sacred or divine by the Mayan and Aztec cultures. Royalty and priests wore their tail feathers during ceremonies. Even today, Guatemala pays homage to the bird by calling its money quetzals.

What makes the quetzal extra-special for me is the personal story that goes with it. I saw one in the Cerro de la Muerte (Mountain of Death) along the Pan Am Highway in Costa Rica. I was staying with Lou and Anne Layman and a small group of others at a comfortable lodge owned by a frenetic, colourful guy who also served as the lodge's bird guide. A stream full of trout passed right by the lodge and the owner reminded us daily that we could have fresh-caught trout, cooked by a master chef, for breakfast, lunch, and/or dinner. I did.

As a bird guide, Armando was unique. He carried a small, palm-sized mirror with him on our bird walks. If a bird was camouflaged against a tree trunk or high up in the thick canopy, he would find a shaft of sunlight and use the mirror to reflect up on the bird, putting it in the sunny spotlight. That's how I saw my first quetzal after much searching: spectacularly spot-lighted on the end of a reflected sunbeam.

Armando's most endearing quality, however, was not his reliability in finding birds, but his enthusiasm. If we were relaxing or scattered around the lodge, he would run crazily through the grounds announcing that a worthwhile bird had just been spotted. One afternoon, an American Dipper made an unexpected appearance. It's a drab, grey bird with a unique behaviour; it searches for food underwater in fast-moving mountain streams. (Yes, you read that correctly: a bird— not a duck—walking purposefully and assuredly underwater!) Armando ran hither and yon yelling in his heavily accented Spanglish, "Eets a Deeper! Eets a Deeper!" I'll remember that scene as long as I live.

We couldn't understand what Armando was saying, but we were captivated by his energy. In seconds, we were all chasing him down the river. He already had his tiny mirror in hand, had found a glint of sunlight, and was focusing a beam of light on some rocks on the far side of the river. A chunky, grey bird walked confidently off the rock and into the swirling stream. Now we understood Armando's excitement. An American Dipper was doing its thing: dipping under the water and walking assuredly against the current! It was as if the bird had magic suction cups on its feet.

Finding a rare bird—a bird that isn't supposed to be in the place you're in or a bird that doesn't get seen very often because its numbers have been drastically reduced or because it's in an inaccessible place—is the birding equivalent of finding a truly exceptional dinosaur bone, or an ancient Roman coin, relic, an old stamp or antique.

It's a delightful moment, a thrilling moment.

You feel like the planets have somehow aligned in your favor, the birding gods have bestowed an unexpected gift on you—a fabulous bird, like something out of a fable.

Hummingbirds
A Divine Pash

It doesn't take too much imagination to see that birds are descendants of dinosaurs. What baffles me is how Archeopteryx, the original avian dinosaur, the "Ur-vogel," evolved all the way down to—or up to—the hummingbirds. I can see the 150-million-year link between the original avian dinosaurs and ostriches, emus, and even albatrosses and kiwis. The connection between Archeopteryx, this giant, ugly, prehistoric bird, and hummingbirds, however, seems impossible.

That's what makes me think (I'm no evolutionary biologist) that hummingbirds might be rare visitors from another planet. Or they might be secret military drones created by some extra-terrestrial Lady Gaga channelling Salvador Dali and Fabergé. If earthly, they seem to have evolved from a cross between a bee and the lint created by a berserk clothes dryer after a tangle with a wildly coloured Peruvian dress and lots of loose sequins.

Hummingbirds are wondrous creatures, but I was a hummingbird-deprived kid. Maybe they were around, but I can't remember ever seeing one. This is not necessarily a human rights issue, and I'm not looking for financial compensation. But, to see a child's eyes light up when he or she sees their first hummer, is to remind me of just what I've missed. They just can't believe their eyes as they see one flitting from one flower to another at Assiniboine Park in the late summer. Spotting another, and another, they are gob-smacked! It's a treasured memory. Hummingbirds are perfect birds for kids.

My first sighting of a hummingbird, or at least my earliest, most vivid and indelible memory of one, happened one magical day in late April, 1972, in Amherst, Massachusetts.

A motley group of ten or fifteen members of a birdwatching course were traipsing through Amherst's West Cemetery looking for returning warblers and such. We'd spotted some Juncos, White-throated Sparrows, and over-wintering birds. Not terribly exciting stuff until someone let out a yelp: "Hummer!" And there it was, a brilliant male Ruby-throated Hummingbird buzzing among the flowers set out around the tombstones.

When we'd entered the cemetery, our guide had immediately taken us to Emily Dickinson's resting place. The hummingbird spotter mentioned that one of her most famous poems is about a hummingbird, and she wondered whether this hummingbird was the spirit of Emily D. I winced and bit my lip. I'm not a believer in this kind of "spiritual" stuff. But I have to admit that the occasion was magical for me. I almost felt like a five-year-old must feel when he or she first spots a hummer. Wow!

I'll admit that I don't always fully understand Emily D's poetry, but her words regarding hummingbirds do strike a chord: "A Route of Evanescence / With a revolving Wheel / A Resonance of Emerald / A Rush of Cochineal." Hmmmm! The colours are right—emerald on the back and a cochineal gorget (a red throat and breast cover—look it up). The nouns are suggestive and the alliteration interesting. As for "Evanescence"—that's a perfect word for hummers. They are so agile and fast that they seem to vanish into thin air—a shimmering flash of colour one moment and then nothing. They're like hockey pucks on American TV. Remember when one of the US networks tried putting a comet-like tail on the puck to help non-hockey fans follow it? Sometimes I think hummingbirds should leave a trail of fairy dust behind so that we can catch up to them.

I feel sorry for people who grow up in hummingbird-free zones, i.e., anywhere outside the Americas. They are *our* birds. I was made aware of this near Patagonia-Sonoita Creek Preserve in southern Arizona, at a famous backyard where I met birders from all over Europe and Asia. Fourteen sugar feeders were hung about the yard, all numbered. Someone would yell out "Costa's at number six," and all the binoculars would move in tandem to that feeder. Or "Blue-throat at ten." And "Wow! Calliope at four. Rare one. Rare one! Calliope at four." There was great excitement in the air—and great camaraderie; many people were seeing hummers for the very first time. I sat in a comfortable lawn chair for hours, drinking a coke from the homeowner's vending machine, marvelling at the antics of these feisty little birds, and sharing stories with people from India, Israel, England, and Germany.

I saw sixteen different kinds of hummers that day, including that rare Calliope from Mexico. It was my first venture into prime hummingbird territory and one of the most memorable. I've chased these tiny, colourful mites to even farther and more exotic places ever since: Costa Rica, Ecuador, Brazil, Trinidad. It helps that these are nice, warm, un-Winnipeg places.

For a kid from New York State and an adult living in Manitoba—with only one hummingbird (the Ruby-throated) to its credit—Costa Rica was almost too much. Fifty-seven varieties of hummers can be found there. Rancho Naturalista, a great birding lodge in the pre-montane rainforest, has a posted list of over 400 different species of birds seen from its famous, second-storey deck and fabulous set of hummingbird feeders. You can be a completely lazy birder and "tick" scores of birds over morning coffee, afternoon tea, or evening drinks. At my leisure, I counted Violet-crowned Woodnymphs, Green Hermits, Green Thorntails, Violet Sabrewings, and Green-crowned Brilliants. The birds are even more colourful than their names.

But the best birding experiences happen on the trails into the hills adjacent to the lodge. Late one afternoon we were guided to a hummingbird lek where scores of the combative little creatures sang and preened and jousted and buzzed about like crazed teenagers at a rave. Since I didn't know anything about hummingbird "lek-ing," it was a real eye-opener.

We then trudged up to a "hummingbird pool" where a ten- or twelve-foot stretch of a forest stream widened to about four feet of cold, darkened water. To our utter astonishment, hummingbirds would approach this fresh water stream, hover about five or six feet above it for a second or two, and then plummet in. By some miracle, they would struggle up, shake off the water, and zoom away, apparently refreshed—or at least cleansed of the mites and debris collected in a day's work. It was like watching the very private ablutions of a fairy tale or mythic creature: a rare and thrilling treat.

Most amazing of all were the Purple-crowned Fairies and especially the Snowcaps. In the dimness of evening, the iridescent purple colours of the fairies' caps were barely visible, but the luminous white underparts and green backs made identification of these uncommon hummers very easy. The tiny Snowcaps were unmistakeable. Smaller than my thumb and lighter than a Loonie, they seemed to smash into a million deep purple pieces when they hit the water. Their brilliant white caps, tipped forward towards their short bills like a jaunty sailor's, shone in the dusk like powerful, miniscule penlights. Sometimes that was all you'd see.

Costa Rica is nothing compared to Ecuador, however. Some birders call it Hummingbird Heaven. Of the estimated 328 species of hummingbirds (probably the second largest family of birds in the world), Ecuador has 135. When John Weier and I went there, we were lucky enough to spot sixty-two different kinds. However, on our first dedicated hummer search, we missed the extremely rare Black-breasted Puffleg at the Yanacocha Reserve. Of course, fewer than 300 still exist, so we had no great expectations. Besides, our next stop at Tandayapa Bird Lodge more than made up for it.

Tandayapa is probably Hummingbird Central; the area has the highest concentration of hummingbirds in all of Ecuador. The lodge itself has a dozen feeders outside its porches, and the hummingbirds there are as thick as mosquitoes in a Manitoba bog in June. Not quite the concentration of a Biblical plague of locusts, but it seemed so at first. There were so many swarming about at one time and battling each other for feeder supremacy that John (a poet) and I tried to come up with an apt descriptor—like the hummingbird equivalent of a murder of crows: a dazzle of hummingbirds, a sparkle, a frenzy, a whelming, a confetti-swirl, a shattered crayon-box, a rainbow blizzard, a … We gave up. Nothing quite captured the experience. (Google lists "a charm of hummingbirds" as the collective—inadequate.)

Because there were so many of them, because they buzzed around so fast, and because they kept darting in and out of the sunlight, losing their distinctive iridescence, identifying them became an almost impossible task. We just had to sit there, sated, besotted. The easiest to identify was the Booted Racquet-tail. It's a small, emerald green hummer with puffy, white "booties" and a long, elaborate tail (longer than its body). That tail looks like its barbs have been stripped down to just two thin stems (rachises) except for two flat racquets at the very end, as if it's got two dark blue ping pong paddles at the end of long, skinny broomsticks. Its function must be a challenge to all evolutionary biologists.

Since it was raining lightly, I was wearing my fire engine red rain jacket—a mistake, as it turned out. As I rose to head in for dinner, I must have seemed like a giant walking tropical flower. I was immediately swarmed by several hummers. If I were an ornithophobe, I would have freaked! They brushed my face and ears and neck with their blurry wings and long bills. It was thrilling but almost creepy. A priest who had to hear the confessions of Catholic nuns every week once described that drudgery as "being stoned to death with ping pong balls." My experience being mobbed by hummers reminded me of that, but it was far from drudgery. I was ecstatic! I almost felt that I could fly away with them. (I would make a very bad hummingbird!)

The only other hummingbird experience that comes close to this was when I participated in a hummingbird banding project with Sheri Williamson, the Arizonian woman who authored the *Peterson Field Guide* on hummers. After the birds were caught and carefully banded, Sheri handed them to me. I held the tiny mites upside down in the palm of my hand for a second to let them recover. Their glossy feathers felt almost like fur. I could feel the rapid beating of their hearts run through my hand to my own heart and right down to the tips of my toes. That feeling of my own strength and tenderness was akin to the sensations I had holding my infant daughters for the very first time. Overwhelming! I was almost in tears.

After a second or two, I opened my hand and the birds invariably righted themselves, paused on my thumb, and then buzzed away. I must admit I had some second thoughts about participating in the banding. Even a light-weight band, attached to trace the birds in the name of science, seemed an imposition. I imagined them flying lopsided, teetering from the extra weight. I hope we did them no harm.

Some people think hummingbirds are exuberant. I see them as impatient, purposeful little creatures, always in a hurry, darting off to someplace on a direct line, as if buzzed on amphetamines. Though they are sentimentalized on greeting cards and wall hangings, I don't think they're romantic figures at all; they're more tragic-comic—tiny, animated clowns in colourful costumes that belie, perhaps, an inner torment. It's their contradictions that fascinate me: cute but feisty, tiny but energetic, frantic by day and torpid at night, colourful in the sunlight and drab without it.

Any creature that is so beautiful in itself and helps to create beauty in the world (by pollinating flowers) is something to be revered. I suppose I have a passion for hummingbirds. Someone once called it "a divine pash." I don't know where the term comes from, but I'll accept it. Hummingbirds seem to have something of the divine in them, or at least something otherworldly or preternatural.

I'd like to live out my days chasing all 328 hummingbird species in the warm, flower-filled spots in the Western Hemisphere. Even when there are scores of them around me, even when they are easy to see, they are rare beings, the rarest of birds.

Once in a Lifetime Birding Experiences

Broad-winged Hawks
An Unexpected Spectacle

East Africa is amazing! You can run out of exclamation points describing it.

I went there with my wife and twenty-five others on a safari led by Bob Taylor. Bob has organized more than thirty safaris to Kenya and Tanzania. He's an excellent birder, but he knows the people, the places, the birds and the animals of East Africa as well as anybody. So we saw a leopard drag a freshly killed zebra carcass up into an acacia tree five metres off the ground to keep it away from his competitors—lions and hyenas and vultures. Wow! We watched a wildebeest give birth, right in front of our eyes, and then nudge the calf to its feet so that they could rejoin the hundred thousand others on their annual migration—all in the space of thirty minutes. Unbelievable!

We shuddered inside our safari vehicle as a cheetah stampeded a herd of hundreds of zebras and impalas right past us; somehow they saw us in the nick of time, despite the dust and panic, and avoided us by mere inches. Whew!

A female elephant that we surprised at the back end of a line of babies and juveniles snorted, flapped her big ears, and charged our vehicle; she stopped before she got to us, but a couple of days later we gaped in awe at the battered hulk of a Range Rover destroyed by an angry elephant. Thank God for our driver!

We had many memorable, close-up experiences like this, often more than one a day. We saw all the "charismatic megafauna:" huffing and pawing rhinos, angry giraffes battering each other with their long necks, mud-lounging Cape buffalo shooing off elephants from a waterhole, teams of skulking lionesses on the hunt, hippos sleeping against our tent stakes ("Don't arouse them; they wake up miserable and mean!"), elephants picking fruit off of trees right over our tent, so close that we could hear their stomachs growling as they digested the fruit, baboons pounding on our roof, a giant constrictor swallowing a hyrax right outside our dining room, and much, much more.

But some of us came to Africa to look for the birds as well as the animals. And right up there on our list of memorable occurrences was the sight of hundreds of thousands of bright pink flamingos, mostly Lesser but with some Greaters scattered among them, feeding on algae and plankton at Lake Natron in northern Tanzania. With the exception of sentries standing upright and scanning for predators, they were bent over and feeding with their hooked beaks in that odd, upside down way that flamingos graze. There were enough of them to almost fill Transcona, Winnipeg with the real deal, not just the small, plastic ones plunked in the front yards of unsuspecting birthday boys and girls. What is it about huge concentrations of birds that grab hold of our imaginations?

When birders get together to brag or reminisce, they usually talk about the three EXes. Not ex-wives, ex-husbands, or Ex-Lax. No, they're the EXtraordinary birds they've seen, the EXceptional experiences they've had, and the unEXpected birds that have come their way. EXtraordinary birds like the Resplendant Quetzal or the Secretary Bird (looks like a weird cross between a stork and an eagle with a black mullet); unEXpected or rare birds like stray Mississippi Kites or Painted Buntings in Manitoba, both species much farther north of their usual range than anyone would ever imagine.

EXceptional experiences often include the sight of enormous numbers of birds, and not necessarily rare ones. It's not the species that is rare; it's the unforeseen and unrepeatable experience that is rare. These are awesome, awe-inspiring spectacles. Far better than superhero movies on IMAX screens where hundreds of thousands of menacing Stormtroopers attack a small group; we know that these movie hordes are fake—computer-generated. Birding spectacles in real life are on a whole other level (and certainly more enjoyable than the birds in the Hitchcock movie!)

Media stories about birds these days are usually depressing. Bird populations are in serious decline everywhere. So anecdotes about unusual numbers of birds can enliven any birding get-togethers. When someone sees more than 200 loons together on a lake (loons being symbols of melancholic loneliness and usually seen alone or in pairs), it can be myth-breaking—and worth a long, often repeated story.

Even large numbers of smaller birds, passerines, can be staggering. As a group of us crept through an April snowstorm that had cascaded over the Rocky Mountains into the Colorado foothills, we came upon field after field of Horned Larks. So many that it was almost impossible to count them—well into the thousands, surely. They'd clearly been stalled on their migration north and were feeding along the roadside, as larks do, or flitting about in the snow-covered grasses trying to keep from being buried. Not knowing anything about lark migration, whether it happens in small flocks or huge waves, we could only marvel at this rare treat.

It reminded me of the first time I saw a flock of Snow Buntings—over 600 of them in a weedy field southeast of Winnipeg. That was impressive until I realized that this was not all that unusual. Nor was the discovery of seventy-five or so Black-billed Magpies not very far away. I'd never seen more than four or five together before this, usually a family of adults and short-tailed juveniles in June, post-fledging. When we saw a hog farmer tossing pig carcasses into a field, we realized that the magpies were lured in from all over the territory. It seemed a cheat, but we still refer to that place as Magpie City.

In Arizona, I've marvelled at the sight of tens of thousands of over-wintering Sandhill Cranes. The thrill of hearing the enchanting language they speak to each other was matched by the whir of all of those wings taking flight together. At dusk in Caroni Swamp in Trinidad, I sat enthralled as 3,000 Scarlet Ibises flew in packs of two, three, and four dozen birds to their evening roosts, like flaming arrows loosed from a medieval army's bows. They were joined by smaller numbers of white egrets, Cattle and Snowy, and Blue Herons—in the hundreds rather than thousands—and together turned a mangrove island into a giant Christmas tree crammed with brightly coloured garlands. It was so spectacular that it brought some in our party to tears.

Perhaps it was spectacles like this that led hunters in the Middle Ages to play a language game. Between rounds of killing fire they'd dream up names for large groups of birds and animals. You've likely heard of a murmuration of starlings. Or a conspiracy of ravens. How about a merl of blackbirds or a spiral of treecreepers or a confusion of warblers or, most peculiarly, a museum of waxwings? (See ornithologist Bill Oddie's book *A Conspiracy of Ravens: A Compendium of Collective Nouns for Birds* for more.) What we saw in Trinidad was a posse of herons. (I've also seen a vortex of vultures over south Florida and a soar of kites along the shores of Lake Geneva in Switzerland.)

My most unforgettable experience of unexpectedly huge numbers of birds occurred on an annual Hawkwatch in September, 2003. A Hawkwatch is part Citizen Science and part social occasion. Every fall, teams of birders are dispatched to familiar areas to count the number of birds that can be found there, mostly migrating hawks but also other species. One Hawkwatch may not make much difference as Citizen Science. But over time, fluctuations in hawk numbers and migration patterns can help professional scientists.

For years, my assigned area has been "Lynchs Point," named after a campground at the southern tip of Lake Manitoba that only sometimes uses an apostrophe where you might expect one to be. The area includes Delta Marsh and the roads to and from the area. It's a great venue, good for the highest number of species recorded by any team.

George Holland, Janice Smith, and I were having an average birding day when we decided to eat our lunch on a small hillock near the entrance to the campground at Lynchs Point. At this point we'd seen some kestrels, harriers, and Red-tailed, Cooper's, and Sharp-shinned Hawks. The usual suspects. Nothing to get too excited about.

As we lounged in the warm sunshine, gazing lazily skyward, Janice noticed small specks against the wispy clouds almost out of range of our binoculars. We all dropped our sandwiches and perked up. George quickly identified the birds—Broad-winged Hawks, fourteen of them.

It was a perfect day for migration. The wind was out of the northwest and as it crossed the warm prairies and hit the cool edge of Lake Manitoba, it created huge thermals—spirals or funnels of ascending air. The Broad-wings were sailing in from the northwest, hitting the thermals, riding them up to their peak in wide circles, and then gliding on until they had to take wing again. A smart way to fly. Hardly any effort.

When we started to pick up individual hawks entering the updrafts at lower levels, we started some serious accounting. Getting the exact number of hawks spiralling up just near the edge of our binocular range was not easy. We began counting by fives and checking with each other. Thirty-four in one kettle, then an additional forty-seven in another. We decided to delay our departure for other prime spots and just hang out there and count Broad-wings. We thought we were on to something big.

A kettle of 320 hawks spiralled in from the northwest. We had to count by tens. Then another seventy-nine flew over, followed by twenty-four, then twenty-three, and a further hundred. Around 2:30 in the afternoon, 350 went by; we counted them by twenties. We stayed on the hillock for four hours, just fixated on the Broad-winged fly-overs. At one point there were so many specks in the air that we could only count by fifties—this huge kettle of birds, coming out of a thermal on a slow, easy glide, numbered an unbelievable 2,250 hawks. It took a long time to pass over us; it was so stretched out that we were confident we'd made a fairly accurate count. With the cloud cover increasing, cutting off the thermals, the numbers diminished. We could count in the ones and twos. But as we tallied our numbers at the end of our watch, we realized we had counted 3,495 Broad-winged Hawks.

To put this in perspective, the usual average is around six Broad-winged Hawks per year in the entire province during migration. In 1982, only 136 Broad-wings were seen in all of Manitoba; that was the previous high. We had almost thirty times as many Broad-wings as that previous record. Astounding!

We could hardly contain our excitement as we drove on to Delta Marsh. What a completely unexpected discovery! We couldn't wait to tell the other hawkwatchers about our numbers: an unprecedented 3,495 Broad-winged Hawks.

But this made us wonder. Where had they come from? (The boreal forests to the north and west.) Why had we missed them in all the previous years? (Bad timing.) And how do they assemble and decide to migrate together? (Who knows?)

While the number of Broad-wings seen that afternoon was

unprecedented, it was miniscule compared to the numbers seen in the Duluth, Minnesota Hawkwatch on the following Monday. More than 100,000 Broad-wings were counted there. Were "our" birds among them? We can only wonder. Perhaps future ornithology students and birders can come up with an answer.

Fast and Furious Falcons

Buff-breasted Sandpipers migrate through southern Manitoba in late August and early September. But they're not reliable migrants. Some years, almost nobody sees them. So, when word goes to members of the manitibabirds Yahoo! Group that Buff-breasteds are around, I jump.

The site where they're often seen is a sod farm near a bison compound just west of Oak Hammock Marsh. John Weier and I headed there after dinner one fine fall evening. No better companion for birding the marsh than John. He spent the better part of a year there and chronicled his birding experiences in *Marshwalker*.

We spotted the birds, twelve of them, almost immediately.

We weren't the only ones. There were falcons about. We were in for a rare treat.

The first one was a Peregrine. It flew in from the east, the marsh area, at a considerable height. Every other bird in the area shut up and hunkered down. The Peregrine plummeted. It missed the Buff-breasteds. A juvenile, it'd have to get better to survive its first year, the most dangerous one for young Peregrines.

It quickly headed back to the marsh where the ducks were settling in for the night and were easier picking. Ducks don't fly very fast. Sandpipers do. You could say that for falcons, they are fast food.

Minutes after the Peregrine missed, a Merlin darted in. It flew low to the ground and scared up the sandpipers. They wheeled in formation as most shorebirds do, flashing in the late sunlight as they banked and turned in perfect synchronicity. There is something glorious and mesmerizing in the way sandpipers can swirl about at great speed in unpredictable directions without touching as much as a wingtip. Not much else can match their coherence and empathy. They are wondrous to watch.

But the Merlin gave them little heed. Probably sated on mice or Savannah Sparrows. For the Merlin, this was just a strafing run, like a fighter jet swooping low over a beach full of sunbathers. If sandpipers could scream, I'm sure they would have. But they didn't let out a peep. Nor did the Merlin vocalize its shrill "key, key, key" call. It was almost as if the Merlin just enjoyed the confusion and terror it generated.

On the next field over, we spotted a falcon on the ground eating bugs. A warm-brown bird. Another young Peregrine or, could it be, a rare Prairie Falcon. We watched and waited, tense with anticipation.

Suddenly it took wing and banked with its wings spread wide. Aha! The underwing coverts were very dark, almost like wing struts. A Prairie Falcon, kissing cousin of the Peregrine, and just as fast and lethal.

Zoom! It flew low and fast over the sod field; the chase was on. The Buff-breasteds rose and again circled the area in a well-coordinated panic. As acrobatic as they were, they were no match for the falcon, the fastest of all flyers. The chase didn't last long. With hair-trigger reflexes, it flew into their midst, reacting to their every swerve and twitch. In a flash, it grabbed one right out of the air in mid-flight.

The falcon flew to a nearby fencepost. The feathers flew as it feasted. Its lighter, narrower "sideburns" confirmed that this wasn't a peregrine. Prairie Falcon. Gotcha! My first of the year.

Before it was too dark to see anything more, we counted eight falcons. They all tried to get a Buff-breasted meal; some were more persistent than others, swooping back and forth, over and among them with malicious intent. Every chase provided as many thrills for us as all six sequels of *The Fast and the Furious* movie franchise. It was like a dogfight between an F-86 Sabrejet and twelve unarmed MiG-15s. Predator vs prey. With stakes as high as they were in the Roman Colosseum or during wartime combat. Live or die, catch or go hungry.

Each falcon relied on its unmatched speed and agility in the air. The sandpipers played the numbers game, trusting in their remarkable ability to fly in tightly packed formations and believing in the old cliché that there's more individual safety in a large group. The pursuer and the pursued zoomed across the flat terrain in a succession of eye-catching aerial dances.

Only the first Prairie Falcon succeeded. Overall, the falcons were one for eight or ten on the night. The best Major League ball players only hit the ball once every three at bats. I don't know what the average success rate of falcons is, but on this night they were very light hitters.

On the other hand, John and I had hit the jackpot. We'll probably never again see such a series of aerial displays!

A Fall-out of Spring Warblers

Nuclear fall-out is terrible. Follicular fall-out is pretty traumatic (I started losing the top of my head—my hair—in my mid-twenties). Avian fall-out is marvelous. It occurs because passerines (songbirds) migrate at night. When a storm front exhausts them and forces them to stop their journeys in great masses, a fall-out occurs. The morning after a fall-out can be a birder's dream.

I've always been a fair-weather golfer. Heavy winds, a sprinkle of rain, temperature below ten degrees Celsius, wafts of mosquitoes (in Manitoba they should be considered weather) and I'm not teeing up. I expect that I'll teach my grandsons the grand old game of golf someday, but I'm not taking them out to a golf course on a cold, rainy day no matter how much they beg.

Lately, I'm finding fair-weather birding more and more attractive. I guess it started with a bird chase in a canyon in southern Arizona where a rare Flame-coloured Tanager was reported. (It was formerly the Flame-backed Tanager, is now a member of the cardinal family, not the tanagers, and looks like an oriole. Don't ask me.) It was eighty degrees Fahrenheit, twenty-seven Celsius. A perfect day for birding, and we'd already ticked more than seventy birds off our lists. My friend Charlie Rattigan and I pulled up to a woody Bed and Breakfast and asked if they'd seen the tanager. The owner was a grey-bearded Vietnam vet. Before he answered, he invited us to sit down in padded chairs on his patio and have a beer with him. Our resistance lasted one nanosecond.

His wife quickly ladled some grape jelly onto a nearby feeder. As we sat there in the shade, our feet propped up, the cardinal, er, tanager, an unexpected vagrant from the mountains of Mexico, undeterred by Homeland Security, danced through the trees like an errant sunbeam and whistled like a happy sailor. Then he obligingly flew in and supped on the sugary purple blob. He sat there long enough for us to put down our beer bottles, raise our binocs, and get great, long looks. In fact, he was so close we barely needed the binocs. Brilliant, flame-red/orange body, black wings with white lines or spots, a black-streaked back, and yellow-green underside. When he flew off and sat whistling in a tree, we all turned to each other, lifted our bottles, and toasted a life-bird. Ah, life was good! This is what birding should be.

What made me act differently a couple of years later I don't recall. All I can say is that when I decided to head off to a Birding and Breakfast outing one cold May morning, I was acting out of character or, at least, out of the current version of my character. On that day, FortWhyte Alive's thermometer read three degrees Celsius and a fierce, face-chafing wind made it feel colder, especially for May. A dozen intrepid birders showed up. On a good day there can be twenty-five to thirty. Nobody was optimistic.

I have a ready term, courtesy of my daughters, for people who engage in this kind of activity: daffy birdwatchers. On this day I included myself. For some weird, unknown reason I got up at 5:15 am to walk my dog so that I could be at the guided walk by 6:30. In my twenties I knew a woman who refused to go hiking or camping. Her idea of roughing it, she said, was a good motel with a TV. Smart lady.

FortWhyte Alive is a former quarry converted to a nature-education centre surrounded by big box stores and suburban housing. A large, deep pond that attracts migrating waterfowl is its main feature. A quick scan of the water revealed nothing special. A few shivering Canada Geese, some desultory Mallards, teal, shovelers, canvasbacks, and scaup whose paddling feet must have been the warmest parts of their anatomy, and a half-dozen awkward cormorants trying to dry their wings and maintain their balance in the frigid blasts. They must have wondered why they ever came back to "sunny Manitoba."

We birders split into several groups, grumbled like spoiled teenagers, and headed into the surrounding, mostly aspen, "woods."

Our spirits perked up when we encountered more than a smattering of sparrows and thrushes scratching through the undergrowth. Many of us quickly and unexpectedly toted up eight or ten first-of-the-year sparrows. Fox, Harris's, White-crowned, Clay-coloured, etc.—they all stuck to the ground for shelter. The grey and brown birds were back.

Then we started to discover warblers—in bunches. Mixed flocks of early arrivals like Yellow-rumps ("butter butts" to the slangy among us) and Orange-crowned mingling with many other varieties. True spring colours at last: oranges, yellows, greens, sprightly blacks and whites. Our group had fourteen species of flitty, colourful warblers by breakfast. Redstarts fanning their fiery tails. Palm Warblers pumping theirs. Yellow Warblers like ripe, flying lemons. Wilson's—like Yellows but with jaunty black tams. Common Yellowthroats with their odd burglar half-masks. Black-and-whites scurrying up trunks and around branches like creepers or nuthatches. Tennessee Warblers and Nashvilles (I still have to check to see which is which). And the dazzlers: Chestnut-sided, Cape May, Blackburnian, Magnolia. Other groups added Northern Waterthrush, Ovenbird, Blackpoll, and Black-throated Green. Eighteen species of warblers in all (of a possible twenty-four) and eighty-six total species before breakfast was over. A miracle morning.

Foul weather can sometimes be the boon rather than the bane of our birding experiences. The cold and wind had precipitated this warbler fallout. They were everywhere, low to the ground and sluggish from the temperature. No "warbler neck" for us from craning back to see them in the treetops. No missed sightings because they spurted away a millisecond before you got your binocs on them. They were easily spotted because the trees had not yet begun to leaf out. Suddenly, the morning didn't seem so cold.

The fair-weather birders who stayed home missed a surprisingly fruitful morning. Shakespeare was right: fair can be foul and foul can be fair.

Eight Things
I've Seen with My Own Two Eyes

1) Yellow Warblers Nesting

Kids not only say the darnedest things, they also collect the darnedest things. My grandson, Torsten, for instance, collects Scooby Doo comics, and, in fact, anything to do with that TV cartoon show. Me? When I was a kid, I collected bubblegum cards—baseball and football cards, automobile cards, airplane cards, even something called "Look and See" cards, whatever. (My parents threw a Campbell's soup box full of bubblegum cards into the trash when they were down-sizing.) And for a short time, when I was maybe eight, nine, or ten, I collected birds' nests.

Left to my own devices when I was a kid (I had very few "devices"—i.e. no TV, wrist watch, or computer), I was free to roam the undeveloped fields and woods around my house. I discovered many things, including dozens of bird nests. Once they were abandoned and I realized they would not be used a second time, I started collecting them. My mother, sensibly, made me store them in the garage.

Two of my father's bachelor brothers, my uncles Ed and John, loved a good cigar. (Perhaps that's why they were single.) Between the two of them, they went through two boxes of White Owl cigars every month. They gave me the empty boxes; I don't remember why. I used those boxes, painted or wall-papered, to store my collection of bird nests—a robin's nest, a Red-eyed Vireo's, a Red-winged Blackbird's, a Goldfinch's, a House

Wren's, and many more whose memory time has erased. I completely forgot about them when we moved.

My cigar boxes were too small for my favourite nest—that of a Yellow Warbler.

You'd think a Yellow Warbler's nest would easily fit into a cigar box. Their nests are usually only about four or five inches in diameter and maybe three inches tall. But this one was special. It was not one nest but four. Exploring a field with grasses up to my chest, I found the original nest in the fork of a spindly tree about two feet off the ground. Surreptitiously, or so I thought, I checked it every day. By the fourth day of my discovery, there were five eggs in the nest.

Then a cowbird showed up and laid an egg on top of the warblers' five. Cowbirds are parasitic nesters. They don't build or tend their own nests; the female lays her eggs in the nest of another bird, relying on the mothering instincts of the adoptive parent to raise the young cowbirds. Some birds are smart enough to recognize an interloper's eggs and do something about it.

Almost immediately, the warblers I was watching started to build a second nest on top of the first, abandoning their own eggs and covering the parasitic cowbird's. Before they could lay their second clutch of eggs, the cowbird beat them to it. They immediately built a third nest, and even a fourth before they gave up. I collected the nest later that summer and stored it in a shoebox.

Watching that warbler-cowbird battle provided a lesson in the cowbird's avian freeloading and sneakiness contrasted with the Yellow Warblers' persistence and ultimate resignation; their interactions taught me that birds aren't just nature's ornaments. They have fascinating adaptive behaviours.

It wasn't until years later that I realized I might have been implicated in the scheme. My daily presence at the warbler nest might have alerted the cowbird to its location. That more important lesson was late in coming. I've reminded my grandson of that lesson. Sometimes good intentions lead to bad consequences—and not just in birding.

2) Crombec Parenting

On safari with a group led by my friend Bwana Bob Taylor in Kenya and Tanzania in 2005, we usually had the early afternoon to ourselves. We would venture out in our safari vehicles in the early morning in search of birds and animals and then again later in the afternoon. During the heat of mid-day most birds and animals lay low. But there were exceptions, so I kept my binoculars handy at all times. I never knew what would turn up.

As I dozed comfortably in the shade after a huge lunch at Sweetwaters Serena Camp in Kenya, I became aware of a persistent squawking somewhere nearby. A raspy kew, kew, kewk. It took me a while to track it down.

On a branch high in an acacia tree was a rufous bird, about the size of an American Robin and the colour of a Brown Thrasher. It had a streaky throat and a large coral-red bill. The bird just stood on the branch making noise. I had a good, long look at it. Two or three slow checks through my field guide combined with return looks at the obligingly stationary bird finally gave me an ID; it was a juvenile Diederik Cuckoo. I'd never seen an adult before, so this was a good find: a lifer.

As I stared at the bird, a much smaller bird popped up beside it. About three and a half inches long, it was half the size of the cuckoo. Its arrival quieted the cuckoo. Then the reason for the squawking became apparent. It was begging to be fed. A morsel was exchanged, and the smaller bird flew off—before I could get a good look at its markings.

It returned in less than a minute with an insect in its beak. A plain brown bird with almost no tail. Rufous underparts and a rufous face. A quick check of the field guide indicated it was a Red-faced Crombec, a kind of small, African warbler. Another lifer.

With little else to do, I watched this exchange for over an hour. I didn't count, but there must have been at least fifty feedings. The cuckoo chick was noisily insistent and never satisfied. The crombec was working its tail off (so to speak) to feed its adoptive "off-spring."

Cowbirds aren't the only parasite nesters, laying their eggs in another bird's nest and relying on the nest builders to raise their young—cuckoos do it too. Likely the cuckoo chick crowded the crombec chicks out of the nest and dominated the crombec parents.

Cuckoo adults are bullies by proxy. They let their kids do the dirty work.

3) Ospreys Learning

On our first trip to Nova Scotia, my wife and I learned a valuable lesson. Well, many lessons, but I'll stick to just one or two.

I was a graduate student at the time and she was a waitress, and together we had no money and little spare time. On the spur of the moment, we tossed a bunch of clothes and a few supplies into her old Toyota and lit out for Nova Scotia from Amherst, Massachusetts. We had no tent and no money for motels or even campsites, so we took an old parachute of hers for cover. (She was a skydiver with over one hundred jumps. Even after a few lessons, I could never work up the nerve to actually jump out of an airborne plane.)

We figured we'd sleep out somewhere under the stars, and, if it rained, we'd stretch her parachute between a couple of trees and use that as our "tent." As it got dark, we'd look for a lonesome, unpaved road somewhere and hope nobody would hassle us.

We found a perfect isolated spot in northern Cape Breton on our third night. We ate peanut butter and jelly sandwiches and watched the brilliant deep sky until we were too tired to count the shooting stars. It was clear when we crawled into our sleeping bags but in the middle of the night, hour unknown, it started to rain; we quickly secured the parachute between the car door and a tree and ducked under it, but not before it started to pour. A monsoon. We got soaked to the skin and ended up huddled together in her tiny car, shivering. Lesson learned: Nova Scotia is a maritime province! It's not as dry as the postcards. Oh, and parachutes are not very water repellent.

We spent the next day, cloud-free and hot, drying out. We spread everything out in the sun on bushes and tree branches and relaxed on that gently sloping hill next to a lake in northern Cape Breton until even the sleeping bags were dry.

As we lay there, we soon spotted an osprey. As large as an eagle but thinner, with a hooked beak, a crook in the elbows of its wings, and brown and white feathers, it was unmistakable. For a brief while it hovered at eye level about fifty metres away and fifteen metres above the water. Then, tucking its beak downward and folding its wings back, it plummeted like a rock towards the lake. At the last second, it pivoted its talons downward and struck the water. What a spectacular dive! And a successful one. After a couple of seconds, it slowly rose out of the lake, shaking the water off its wings, and flew away with a large fish wriggling in its talons.

A second bird came on the scene almost immediately, before we could really get over the excitement of the first display. It circled a bit, hovered, and then attempted the same maneuver. It, however, came up empty. Perhaps an unanticipated gust of wind blew it slightly off course. Perhaps it hadn't learned the delicate art of subtly adjusting its wings and/or tail to correct the descent. It tried again. Halfway down it aborted the dive, swooping up to scan the water again. It rose up to its original height and coasted along for a couple of minutes, finally dropping three times in small increments to get a better look. Its plunge was short but for some reason unsuccessful. Seemingly frustrated, it flew off in the same direction as its predecessor.

Several long minutes later, another osprey followed. Too enthusiastic, it hit the water and plunged too deeply. It was a hard struggle to break free of the grip of the lake. The osprey flapped and flailed. When it finally wrenched itself out of the water, it too flew away with no lunch.

As we whiled away the hours, it became apparent that we were watching a family (or two) of ospreys fishing. Probably six of them, two adults, male and female, and four juveniles. This must have been a great lake for they came back regularly, scanning, hovering, dropping tentatively or assuredly, swooping back up, and plunging with more failures than successes. Sometimes, whether they met with success or not, they seemed to rest on the water's surface. Then they'd extend their wings and lift off.

One of the adult ospreys adjusted a fish in its talons when it managed a successful catch. It was like a high-wire juggling act. We held our breath to see if the fish, still alive, would wriggle free. The osprey somehow got the fish pointing forward. No juveniles were anywhere in sight. Too bad. They could have learned a simple lesson in prey aerodynamics and osprey "dexterity." We wondered how this skill was passed along.

Watching the ospreys learn was a pleasant way to pass the time. Some fishing attempts were too tentative. Some were too enthusiastic. Some just errant. A couple of times the ospreys dropped the fish that they'd managed to snag. We sat there amused for hours.

Many years later, when I was teaching my daughters how to ride two-wheeled bikes without training wheels and then drive a car, I remembered the ospreys. So far as we could tell, osprey parents are not like twenty-first century human parents, so-called helicopter parents. Osprey adults can hover as they search for fish but they don't hover next to their kids providing show-and-tell lessons. Spotting fish, diving fast and sure, calculating the speed of the target fish and its depth below the water's surface, judging distances, and mastering the art of talon-eye coordination: these are all learned skills. The youngsters had no manuals, and, so far as I could tell, no helping "hand" or nervous advice from the parents. No adult guidance about when and how to hit the water, how to grab and retain a wriggling fish. The ospreys learn at the school of hard knocks. Amazing!

With their casual avian attitude toward parenting, osprey adults are obviously not models for us humans to follow. (But, let's be honest, there are times when we all wish that we were ospreys!) I helped my daughters learn the intricacies of modern life, even enjoyed dealing with their bruised knees and battered egos. I expect I'll offer my fair share of advice, where needed, to my grandsons. I hope I'll get to show them how ospreys fish and learn to fish. Kids need to see the world in all of its splendor.

4) Eagles Fishing

On a sunny Sunday evening in Englishtown, Nova Scotia in 2011, my wife and I stopped at a community centre for their monthly supper. All the codcakes, mashed potatoes, corn on the cob, salad, and homemade bread we could eat plus home-made apple pie à la mode and coffee. For just ten bucks! As we were gorging ourselves and talking to the locals (mostly old folks eager to provide us with the town's history and gossip), two dozen or so Harley-Davidson motorcycles roared up and parked right outside the front door. Maybe thirty tough-looking, leather-clad bikers and biker chicks assembled by the door, cased the place, and walked in. There was a collective gulp from the old folks. The room turned eerily quiet.

It was 7:15. We had been the last people allowed in at 7:05. The place was closed. No more food left. I'm sure we were all thinking the same thing: I wish Jesus were here and could pull off his loaves and fishes miracle one more time!

But the bikers did not tear up the place. They left quietly. We took our time cleaning up the food on our plates, allowing the bikers to re-mount their hogs and get away. We did not go back for seconds on the pie.

We were still stuffed the next morning. Worried about seasickness (neither one of us had been out to sea on a pelagic birding tour before), we debated whether or not we should take a boat trip out into the ocean to see some puffins. We popped a couple of Rolaids each and checked the weather. A perfect day for puffin watching: blue sky, calm waters, tangy, salty sea air.

The bird boat was a re-fitted fishing vessel with a crew of two. Six people (no bikers) joined us for the us for the two-hour round trip, a half hour out, a half hour back, and an hour circling Bird Island. Ten minutes from the dock, the first mate (and captain's wife) appeared on the prow with a bucket of chum. Since we were heading out to see puffins, auks, razorbacks, and kittiwakes, I thought she was going to use the chum to lure the puffins closer to us and the six other camera-toting tourists on board.

Suddenly, the woman gave a piercing wolf-whistle. Two mature Bald Eagles flew out of the nearby forest and alit on bare tree branches along the shore. The woman told everyone to get their cameras ready. Then she flung a huge fish high into the air; too big for puffins, I thought. The fish landed in the water with a distinct plop about ten feet from the boat. "Focus your cameras on the fish," she ordered and gave another whistle. One of the eagles lifted off its branch, zoomed across the water, extended its long legs, and deftly snatched the fish out of the water as cameras clicked. She tossed another dead fish into the water, whistled twice, and the second eagle repeated the scene. "Everybody happy?" she asked. People checked their cameras, cell phones, and iPads. Someone grumbled. So she gave another whistle and a third and fourth eagle appeared and got in on the act.

And that, my ornithological friends, is why so many perfectly focussed photos of acrobatic eagles catching fish are available. Pavlovian raptors! Who knew?

It was only when we got to the island that we realized the full ramifications of this Pavlovian performance. When the Nova Scotia government closed many of the open dumpsites in the province, the eagles that dined there turned their attention to the bird islands. They were now dining on puffins, auks, razorbacks, and kittiwakes or their eggs. In fact, kittiwakes were no longer found on the island we visited. Eagles had stolen their eggs or killed their young. They were like Hell's Angels coming to a small town to terrorize the residents—unlike the quieter bikers who'd scared us all at the community centre. The tour boat had at least found a way to lure four eagles away from feasting on easy-to-catch seabirds. And groups of tourists got perfect pictures of eagles grabbing fish to show to their friends. Win, win.

5) Eagles Hunting

One lazy afternoon I spotted two mature Bald Eagles perched in the tall cottonwood trees on the west side of the Red River at the edge of Kings Park in Winnipeg. Below them, about a dozen Mallards floated nervously. Suddenly, one of the eagles swooped down at them. The ducks all quickly dove underwater. The eagle missed and returned to its perch. But as the ducks resurfaced, the other eagle swooped down at them. Although it hardly seemed like enough time to catch their breath, the ducks dove again. The second eagle missed. It too returned to its perch and the ducks popped up again. But they refused to fly away. I guess they feared they'd be easier targets on the wing.

So the eagles repeated their double-teaming forays. One would swoop down. The ducks would dive. The ducks would resurface. And the second eagle would go at them. This was repeated maybe ten times over the next several minutes. It was quite an amusing show.

Were the eagles simply inept at this kind of double-whammy hunting? (What is a "whammy," by the way, before it is doubled?) Was one eagle, already sated, simply teaching another the tricks of the trade? Or were they playing an elaborate game? Can birds have fun?

I've seen a pair of eagles cavort in the sky, locking talons and tumbling through the air as if they were avian thrill-seekers or members of a Cirque du Soleil troupe. Is this fun? Or are they just following basic naturalistic urges? How much play is there in raptor foreplay? Is there pleasure in this mating *game*? Interesting questions, eh?

If the double-teaming eagles were just having fun, just playing at hunting, it was a particularly sadistic kind of game. Perhaps this kind of behaviour is what Ben Franklin observed when he proposed the turkey instead of the eagle as the American national symbol. Eagles, he thought, had "bad moral character."

6) Geese Whiffling

My friend Charlie Rattigan's parents, Lee and Big Charlie, used to organize a Goosewatch every spring. At dawn on an April Sunday, in a ritual almost as formal as a Catholic Mass, about a dozen of their friends would assemble a convoy and head to Montezuma Swamp, a stopover for migrating birds in central New York State. It was the Rattigan's way of celebrating the return of spring.

By 8:00 am or so, we would all be parked at the edge of a grove of Cottonwood trees and have arranged several barbecues around the picnic tables there. Snow banks still filled the shadows, and the air was usually nippy, but that just added to the festive occasion.

Some of the more serious birders would check the ponds for the water birds that had already arrived: Mallards, teal, canvasbacks, shovelers, etc. The usual suspects. If something unusual was found, everybody would traipse over for a good look.

Then the designated cooks would begin to prepare eggs and toast on the grills and try to heat up jars of Hollandaise sauce. Eggs Benedict—a delicious outdoor treat even though the toast was often burnt, the eggs runny or overcooked, and the sauce lukewarm. Some would opt for tepid instant coffee, but most of us would stand in line waiting for Lee to break out her bottles of homemade champagne. What a feast!

The picnic tables were arranged perpendicular to the nearby pond so that all parties could see the geese land and watch them approach through the leafless trees. Because the trees were so close to the water and the pond so narrow, the geese could not approach like jetliners approaching a long airport runway. They could not slowly glide in on a decreasing hypotenuse. They could not slide onto the water with their wide feet and ski to a halt.

The geese, all Canadas, would get to the edge of the cottonwood trees about fifty feet above the water and whiffle down. They'd bank sharply and swoop back and forth in a perpendicular drop. You could hear the sound of the wind sifting through their feathers.

If it was a large flock, they'd sometimes bump into each other on the way down. Then they'd hit the water with a plop.

The first time I saw it, I was mesmerized by their odd acrobatics. I've seen whiffling geese only occasionally in the succeeding years. On the prairies there are few obstructions—geese plane in gracefully and slide on their webbed feet as if they're on water skis.

I realize now that watching the whiffling geese was just an excuse for a communal Eggs Benedict and champagne social. The Goosewatch was an amusing spring ritual. I miss it. The closest we come in Manitoba are the Birding and Breakfast outings at FortWhyte Alive on Wednesday and Friday mornings in late April and May. A ninety-minute walk along the lakes, past the buffalo meadows, and through the aspen, willow, and spruce forest is followed by a communal breakfast. No homemade champagne, I'm afraid, but a great way to get your day going and celebrate the arrival of spring.

7) Redpolls Snuggling

It was one of those abysmally cold winter days that most sane Manitobans dread, even the ones who think they're completely winterized. There was a gusty wind that could chafe every layer of skin right off your face if you didn't cover up. Wind chill: minus one thousand degrees Celsius or so. Super crunchy snow underfoot. Three suns—the real one and two adjacent sundogs—sat low in the afternoon sky. They seemed to be there just to mock me. "We'll provide some brightness, you poor slob, but no warmth at all!"

Long johns, jeans, ski pants, thermal undershirt, flannel shirt, fleece, parka, tuque pulled down over my eyebrows, scarf pulled up over my chin, mouth, and nose. Only my eyes exposed, with frost forming on my eyelashes after two or three steps.

Walking my dog Buddy that morning absolved me of all my many sins. No fast trip to hell for me, this was hellish enough. I'd earned a pass. The afternoon walk meant I'd moved to the front of the line in purgatory too.

These were the days before the white birch plague purged the neighbourhood of my favourite tree. With the birches gone, the redpolls too became less frequent presences. Redpolls love birch trees.

So, halfway through my walk, when I heard their familiar twitter and saw a small flock flitting about, I was pleased. The red spot on their foreheads, like a jauntily tilted French beret, always grabbed my attention. They immediately cheered me up. And made me wonder: How do these seemingly frail little birds survive our punishing winters? Do they grow an extra layer of fat? It didn't seem so; they didn't look bulked up at all. Do they fluff out their feathers for insulation? This seemed impossible in the bitter wind. They hardly seemed equipped to cope.

As I trudged along the Red River behind St. Amant Centre, I watched as a redpoll seemed to disappear into a thicket behind an ash tree with a dilapidated Wood Duck nesting box hanging from it. Then another one vanished. Hmmm. I walked closer.

Bob Taylor once told me about finding a Screech Owl nest cavity full of shivering chickadees one frigid day. It seemed like a bad idea to Bob, as if they were tempting fate. They were warding off the cold, but what if the owl decided to return to its cavity? It could feast for days on a banquet of chickadees, delivered right to its door.

To see something so special you have to be acutely observant, very patient, or damn lucky. I was very jealous. Bob was both observant and patient. He knew more about bird behaviour than anybody I knew. Walking Buddy on that bitter January day, I got lucky. I cautiously approached the old nesting box, paused, and then slowly and carefully lifted the lid. What was in there? A huddled ball of feathers. About a dozen redpolls were snuggling together for warmth. In three layers, I think. I guess they were too small and light to squash or smother each other. Luckily, they paid me no heed.

Later, I found out that redpolls, like chickadees, regularly resort to "communal roosting" of this sort to ward off the wind and cold. They can even burrow into snow banks for shelter—in the hundreds and the thousands. They evidently shift positions every once in a while so that no one gets to spend the entire night on the outside layer or at the very bottom. I didn't stick around to check.

Once, in Costa Rica, I found what looked like a black, furry animal curled up in a large basketball-sized clump on a bare tree branch. It turned out to be a cluster of anis. They didn't seem to need to jam together for warmth; it was a hot, tropical February day. They just liked each other, I guess. Maybe they were canoodling. Very chummy birds, anis.

Likewise, the Speckled Mousebirds in Tanzania. These small brown birds with long tails and unmistakable crests also cluster together on warm days. There must not be a mousebird phrase for "I need my own personal space, Mac!"

Instead, the redpolls I saw were bunched up out of necessity. Smart little birds.

8) Horned Larks Larking

Winters can be rough here in Manitoba. The only way to beat them, I've learned, is to not let them beat you down. Get outside every day. Go birding when you can. Believe it or not, over one hundred species of birds are sighted in this province during an average winter.

One February, two young grad students from Europe asked me to take them on a dead-of-winter bird outing. Since they were from Spain and southern Italy, they had never birded in the severe cold. It was nearly minus forty Celsius, grey, and blustery when we went out. They were wary but as excited as kids on their way to Grandma's house on Christmas Eve.

The birds on that particular day were few and far between: crows and ravens, some woodpeckers and nuthatches and chickadees, a handful of hardy House Sparrows and a small flock of pigeons. What made it memorable were the four owls we spotted: a Great Horned Owl, a Screech Owl, and, best of all, a Snowy Owl and a Great Grey Owl. I made them get out of the warm car and trudge through the snow to get better views of the latter two—lifers for them both. The Snowy was a mature male, almost pure white, sitting on the snow and whiter than its surroundings. That's how I spotted it. The Great Grey was perched on a hydro pole, its big, yellow eyes watching us every step of the way as we cautiously approached. I pointed out the characteristic markings—oversized head, little white beard (more of a goatee), white semi-circles between the eyes. But I didn't need to as they'd come well-prepared. They were so excited that they laughed as we walked back to the car and continued laughing all the way back to a Tim Horton's where we had celebratory donuts and large cups of welcome hot chocolate.

What made the trip a bit disappointing was a lack of larks. Larks are my favourite winter birds.

I used to jump in my car on the first clear, snow-free day in early February (on or near an accompanying friend's birthday) and head southwest of Winnipeg to find Horned Larks. Onto the bald-headed prairie—the snow-covered terrain as flat and subtly featured as a rice cake. On a good day, we'd find a Snowy Owl or two, regular winter visitors, or rafts of Snow Buntings, migrants from farther north. We always saw them as reminders that things elsewhere could be worse. Larks reminded us that things weren't as bad as they might seem.

Horned Larks are slender, slightly smaller than robins, with tawny bodies and distinct facial markings. The "horns" are not like a cow's or a horned toad's. They are small, black, feathery protuberances at the upper sides of the head. Sometimes they are barely visible.

Larks are not the true harbingers of spring the way swallows are to San Juan Capistrano, California and vultures are to Hinckley, Ohio, or robins are for the average citizen. Larks don't qualify because some of them over-winter here. And the ones that migrate usually come back far ahead of the official arrival of spring on March 21, and certainly well before the snow melts (the actual arrival of our spring, sometime in April). But when I'm lucky enough to find them, I like to celebrate their hardiness.

Any bird, especially one so delicate, one that sticks around on the wind-raked prairies from November to March or comes back here in the dead of winter has got to be special. These birds deserve a salute, a toot of the horn, as they flit along the road edges, folding their wings after each beat or two, and never flying very high or far from the car. Larks larking about. For my friend, each year they were a true birthday gift, much cheerier than all the candles on his birthday cake.

Bob Nero
and the Great Grey Owl

Manitoba is famous for its winter owls. People come from all over the world to see Great Grey Owls, Northern Hawk Owls, and Snowy Owls in our province. But winter owling can be frustrating. Some years, these "big-three" winter owls are plentiful and can be easily found; other years almost nothing. In a very good year, birders can spot these much sought-after raptors within an hour of Winnipeg. Once they come down from the north or out of the boreal forest, these owls pretty much stay put for the winter wherever they settle in. And they are diurnal, i.e. they hunt during the day. Finding them can sometimes be surprisingly easy.

One winter I was lucky enough to record a six-owl day—six different kinds of owls in one fantastic afternoon. I had great views of the big-three visiting owls from the north plus the more sedentary and year-round owls: a Great Horned Owl, a Barred Owl, and an Eastern Screech Owl. It was one of the most satisfying days of my birding life—until I chanced on the renowned expert on Great Grey Owls, wildlife biologist Bob Nero.

Although the Great Grey Owl was one of my target birds when I first came to Manitoba in 1974, I didn't actually see one until the late 1980s. And that owl was not a wild bird, not anymore. It was Lady Gray'l, the tamed owl that Bob Nero rescued in 1984 and took to various venues to educate the public about owls. With its big, yellow eyes, broad, round face, white chin patches (like a beard), and lack of ear-tufts or "horns," she was a real beauty. Lady Gray'l sat on a perch so still and unruffled, she appeared at first to be a taxidermal specimen. It was when she slowly turned her head that she startled people, myself included. I had to catch my breath!

Once I saw this captive owl, I knew I had to find one in the wild. I saw several "plunge" marks in the snow before I saw my first actual Great Grey. These birds have extraordinary hearing. Their favoured prey, voles, usually scurry through tunnels under the snow. The owls stare down from a high perch, focussing their ears on the snow below. When they hear a vole, they plunge downward, leaving noticeable impressions where their spread wings and talons hit the snow. Plunge marks don't always signal successful forays.

One of the most memorable birding experiences of my birding life happened on a Sunday afternoon a couple of years after my six-owl day. I was in a carful of owlers and we chanced upon Bob Nero's familiar Subaru wagon in perfect owl territory. There wasn't much snow that winter and the owls had come to the edge of the boreal forest to hunt. It was a calm and cloudy day—perfect for seeing Great Grey Owls.

Bob and his long-time banding partner, Herb Copland, were sitting in the front seat of Bob's green Subaru. Curious, we stopped behind them and silently gathered around their car. Bob was behind the wheel. On his lap, he was holding what we'd all hoped to see—a supine, un-protesting Great Grey Owl. Its fierce talons were caught in Bob's firm grasp; its head was covered by a funny white toque. Herb handed Bob a small, silvery ring. In one deft and sudden move, Bob crimped the band on the owl's left leg and read aloud the coded number, one that Herb entered into a well-thumbed logbook.

We backed off as the two of them left the car and met each other by the driver's-side headlight. There, Bob swiftly removed the owl's toque and dipped the owl head-first into one leg of a ragged pair of pantyhose. In the tight pantyhose, the owl shrunk to half its size. It was not nearly as big as it looked, with more than half of its sizable bulk composed of poufy feathers.

Herb hung the pantyhose on the hook of an old scale. A healthy bird— about three pounds. Once it was weighed and recorded, Bob pulled the un-objecting owl, talons first, from its nylon, constricting pouch like an old-time magician gracefully extracting a bouquet of thorny-stemmed roses from his magician's top hat. He turned the owl erect. It blinked its yellow eyes. We all held our breath in the stifling cold.

With a showman's sense of the moment, Bob motioned us to gather around him. We did, but slowly. I remembered what a Great Horned Owl once did when I was a TV production assistant. The on-air biologist lost his focus on the bird less than six feet in front of me. The owl's talons carved eighty stitches worth of gouge marks into his arm! Blood spurted everywhere. I never want to see that again.

Pushing his glasses back up his nose, Bob stared directly into the owl's big, yellow eyes. He then calmly bowed his head before the owl as if in abject submission. Mere inches from the raptor's flexing, sharp talons. As if on cue, the disarmed bird leaned over and gently combed the thinning, white hair on Bob's head. Once, twice, three times, the owl stroked Bob's forehead.

We were all stunned, gasping silently. Afraid to clap or laugh lest we startle the owl and provoke a bloody climax to this unexpected roadside drama, we just stood there, mouths hanging wide open in astonishment. The owl's strong, sharp beak could have split Bob's scalp right to the bone! It was a moment, perhaps more, frozen in time, now firmly packed into our memories.

Finally, Bob turned his back on us and lowered his arm. The owl visibly tensed and spread its wings. Bob loosened his grasp on the owl's legs and the majestic bird took flight. With slow and silent wingbeats, it made its way to a bare branch where it ruffled its feathers and stared back at us in what could have been owlish disdain, its dignity seemingly restored. We all noisily exhaled.

We were so flabbergasted (my flabber had never been so gasted before) by the event we'd just witnessed that none of us could talk sensibly. No one had the presence of mind to ask Bob how he first discovered this grooming "trick." Had he tried it before on any one of the more than 1,000 owls he'd previously banded? Perhaps he'd learned it from his avian friend and companion, Lady Gray'l. All I know is that I'd been witness to one of the most extraordinary demonstrations I'll ever see. By the world's expert on Great Grey Owls, the man almost single-handedly responsible for convincing Manitoba's politicians to make the Great Grey Owl the province's official bird symbol. What a thrilling, un-erasable memory!

Churchill, Manitoba
A Birder's Chilly Paradise

Whenever I hear a non-Manitoban complain about the cold, I think of the famous knife scene in *Crocodile Dundee*.

Aussie outbacker Mick Dundee is adrift in New York City when a mugger attacks him with a knife and demands his wallet. I haven't seen the movie in years, but I can still remember Mick's classic line. He pulls out his own oversized Bowie-style knife, points at the would-be mugger's puny little shiv, and says, "That's not a knife." Then he smiles and brandishes his own weapon. "THAT'S a knife!" He out-blades the mugger who quickly scurries away. (Freudians take note.)

We Manitobans think of our winters in the same terms. "You call that cold? That's not cold. We'll give you COLD!"

How cold is it here? It's so-o-o cold … (insert your favourite David Letterman or Johnny Carson joke here).

I used to think that Winnipeg at its coldest was as bad as it could ever get. Then I went to Churchill, Manitoba. In late June no less. 1984.

Winnipeg, when I left, was hotter than the hinges of Hell. After a three-hour plane ride north, I figured it would be a bit cooler. Little did I know.

As the plane swung low over the delta of the Churchill River, we could see that the harbour and Hudsons Bay were ice-free. What initially appeared to be thirty or so white cigars just below the surface of the water turned out, on closer inspection, to be belugas. My first thrill! I could hardly wait for a better look.

The plane swung out over the bay, the rusty-brown wreck of an old freighter, and, on the rocks at the north end of the runway, a bellyflopped DC-3. (Someone later said it was overloaded with Coke cans headed farther north when it came down.) I hardly had a chance to process the crash when our plane landed with a clatter of stones on the gravel runway. I didn't inspect the undercarriage for pockmarks or pinholes from the gravel when I deplaned.

When we arrived, the temperature was fairly mild. Then, overnight, the wind changed direction, shaking the windows of the lodge as it blew in from the northeast. In the morning, icebergs clogged the harbour and filled the bay as far as the eye could see. The wind chill must have been well below minus fifty! I put on a t-shirt, flannel shirt, sweat shirt, and parka, and it wasn't enough. We were so cold that when we described ourselves as "intrepid," the word sounded more like "stupid." When we spoke, our words crashed to the ground and broke into a thousand icy pieces.

Despite the cold, we did spot over one hundred species of birds. Black-bellied Plovers so sated on wild berries that they just sat stock-still on the ground as you approached them within a foot or so. Most of us had first-time-ever sightings. Jaegers flying overhead. Willow Ptarmigan in mid-molt—changing from their all-white winter plumage to their brown camouflage of summer. Both kinds of Eiders, Common and King, bobbing offshore, although whether we'd actually seen a King Eider was a matter of some dispute. But since this was the end of June, and the midnight sun kept Churchill in daylight around the clock, we could finish a full day's birding with a lively dispute over drinks at mid-"night." King Eider, yes, as well as Common Eiders. The more fanatical in our group became almost round-the-clock birders. If you worry about sleep-deprivation, don't go birding at Churchill in late June.

The most spectacular sighting of the trip was a pair of Ross's Gulls. A dainty white gull with a rosy-hued breast and belly, this gull is native to northern Asia but has chosen the Churchill area for its breeding home for several years. It's a target bird for birders from all over the world and its nest was being carefully monitored by volunteers from the World Wildlife Fund so that collectors would not sneak in and poach its precious eggs.

We saw the birds regularly, but one memorable morning walk on the pebbled beach of the bay stands out. A male Ross's Gull flew over and around us within touching distance as we got ourselves dizzy trying to photograph it in close-ups. Was it curious about our well-parkad and toqued group? Or maybe searching for a hand-out? We'll never know. All we'll know is that this close encounter with an alien bird couldn't have been more of a treat.

In 1984, Tundra Buggies had just arrived in Churchill but they were not yet ferrying tourists around the area. On Cape Mary, a ranger accompanied us on our bird walk, a loaded shotgun at the ready in case a polar surprised us. Later we took an old van to the town dump (now closed), and watched a couple of hungry polar bears, blackened with soot from burning garbage, scavenge for food. Black polar bears! Some with orange circles spray-painted on their backs denoting troublesome bears. Repeat offenders were locked in the polar bear jail. Not what we'd expected.

Nor was the balmy weather we got at the end of our visit. With winds out of the south, the temperature rose to plus thirty! From minus fifty to plus thirty in a week! People from town were sailboarding on the now (mostly) ice-free ponds. It was so warm that Bob Shettler, a seemingly sober-sided engineer, unexpectedly stripped down and dove into the still-frigid Churchill River. "Now I can say I swam north of the Arctic Circle," he chattered as he emerged from the water. I took my boots and socks off and slowly inched in. My feet went numb. I feared they'd they'd suffer irreparable damage. Thirty years later I can still feel the cold!

The hot temperatures brought out the bugs. We had to cover every square centimetre of potentially exposed skin against their stinging onslaught with mosquito netting, bug spray, two layers of clothing, anything available. Everyone walked with an aura of mosquitoes and black flies around them, swarms of bugs a foot thick, visible from a distance. The buzzing from the bugs was so loud and unceasing that townspeople wore earplugs to dampen the noise. Using binoculars was almost impossible.

Twenty-five years after this trip, my wife and I flew up on Halloween Eve to see the polar bears and maybe some birds and animals I'd missed before. Churchill had changed dramatically. From a few buildings huddled around the municipal centre, it had become a small tourist town. We boarded one of a dozen Tundra Buggies and lumbered out to Polar Bear Alley where most of the bears waited for the bay to freeze over. Fierce winds (70 kph) prevailed for most of the day and snow swirled about frequently, creating almost white-out conditions. Though the bears were mostly hunkered down in the bushes, we did manage to see seven bears up close (two weighed about 1,000 kilograms each and stood six feet at shoulder) and two Arctic foxes. On the windless day before, people had seen over thirty bears and many lingering birds, but today there was "grease ice" all around Gordon Point where the shorebirds had been spotted, including a Purple Sandpiper that I'd hoped to see. The shorebirds and ducks (especially the Brants, top on my must-see list) had sensibly departed south.

Still, our one-day visit was memorable. We got to see small gangs of costumed Churchill kids trick-or-treating though town with shotgun-toting guards watching out for trick-or-treating polar bears. (No one wore a polar bear or seal costume.) And we ended the day with an Arctic char dinner with all the fixins at The Churchill Hotel. We skipped the dog sled and Skidoo rides, the helicopter flyovers, and a night at the Tundra Buggy Lodge (a Tundra Buggy with bunks). Churchill is truly a wonder of the world. Even a day there without many bird sightings makes the trip well worth taking..

The Big Spit
At a Birding Festival

Ninety bird species in one day. Eight lifers in four days. That's what a good bird guide can get you, even if you're an experienced birder. And that's what birding festivals can provide: a chance to hook up with bird guides who are local experts. Even if you aren't able to join the guides, you can always follow their itineraries and find some birds on your own.

Plus you get a chance to check out the latest optics, apps, artwork, birding publications, destinations, and tours. And an opportunity to listen to nationally recognized speakers (like Richard Crossley of *The Crossley ID Guide* series and James Currie of *Birding Adventures TV*) as well as participate in birding seminars and workshops.

With thousands of participants, the Space Coast Birding and Wildlife Festival in Titusville, Florida is among the biggest and considered to be among the best in America. Because it's so big (around 4,000 registrants, I heard), you'd better sign up early for everything, especially the field trips. I was at a cruel disadvantage here: I didn't check things out until I got there—the day before it officially opened. By then, most of the bird outings that I wanted to join were full. No room on the bus for North Brevard Hotspots, the St. Johns National Wildlife Refuge, the Ritch Grissom Memorial Wetlands at Viera, or Zellwood and Lake Apopka. Although I mapped out the general itineraries of all of these trips and went there on my own, I was birding blind. I saw none of my target birds, birds that the experienced guides familiar with the territory could easily find.

No Black Rails, no Gull-billed Terns, no Black-necked Stilts, no

Short-tailed Hawks, no Grasshopper Sparrows, no Vermillion Flycatchers. And on and on. No. No. No.

Local knowledge can be crucial for finding birds. It's one thing to go to a wildlife refuge. It's quite another to know that in this small grove of trees, at this particular time of day, behaving in this characteristic way, calling rather than singing, you will find this particular bird. A bird guide can provide those insider tips.

Still, even though I was late signing up and missed out on what I'm sure were incredible birding adventures, it was a fruitful experience, both for me and for my lifer list." [I've taken "still" from the second line of your sentence and used it to introduce the paragraph.

They call Florida a peninsula, but it's just a giant sandbar. A friend of mine calls it The Big Spit. My original plan was to go there for the winter—toss my binocs, my bird guides, my bathing suit, my golf clubs, and my dog into my camper and head south for a couple of months. Ah, warmth. I was really looking forward to being roasted brown.

Well, those plans went out the window.

Then I got an invitation from my long-time friend Charlie Rattigan to join him at the aforementioned Space Coast Birding and Wildlife Festival. I knew nothing about the festival, but it was in an area where I could finally, maybe, find the Florida Scrub-jay, a bird that had eluded me on three previous trips to The Sunshine State. Maybe the Red-cockaded Woodpecker and the Brown-headed Nuthatch too.

Only one week in Florida instead of two months: I'd better make the most of it.

We got to Titusville a day before the festival began and decided to do some preliminary birding on our own. Using the Audubon Bird Guide app with its "Find Birds with eBird" connection on Charlie's iPhone, we quickly found out where Florida Scrub-jays had recently been spotted. Of the numerous sightings, Canaveral National Seashore seemed like the perfect choice; it was not only close but also shared a border with Merritt Island National Wildlife Refuge.

When we got to the fee station on Merritt Island, we asked the ranger on duty where the Scrub-jays were. An affable, talkative guy, he told us to park the car and walk behind the ranger station. We couldn't believe it. They could be right there!

Then again, the curse of the mythical Florida Scrub-jay could still be operational. I'd missed a *sure thing* before; I could be unlucky again.

Before we began walking around, we checked the app for the songs and calls of the jay. Not as noisy and insistent as a Blue Jay. Quieter, a more modest "shreep."

Right away, we saw a jay-sized, grey-ish bird scooting through the bushes. Could we be so lucky as to see a Scrub-jay this quickly?

Nope. It was a Northern Mockingbird (very plentiful in Florida).

Was that a "shreep" we heard on the other side of the bushes? Was that the mockingbird mocking us, imitating the jay?

We cut though the bushes and got to an opening where the railroad tracks separated the refuge from the Kennedy Space Center. We'd been warned not to go past the tracks. Homeland Security, don't ya know. For a second I thought to myself: am I willing to be clapped in jail for a lifer? Will I have to cross the tracks to find the elusive Florida Scrub-jay?

In the time it took to ask and answer my own question, it became irrelevant. A Scrub-jay appeared as if out of nowhere, flying across the tracks from the Space Center property and perching in a small tree next to the tracks. Then suddenly another, and another, and another. Four Scrub-jays. Three hopping on the tracks, coming ever closer. We hoisted our binocs and took them in. Soon we didn't really need to. The jays were close enough to see them clearly with the naked eye. These are lovely birds: a blue that reminds me of the colour of a Mountain Bluebird with a white throat and a necklace of blue.

Scrub-jays are curious and fearless like their cousins the Grey Jays, the "Whiskey Jacks." The boldest one, with four leg bands, bounced along the railroad ties and came within a foot of my boots. The three others, without bands, got within six feet or so, but no closer. The jays stayed until we had imprinted them indelibly in our minds. What a great way to get a lifer!

On our way out, we thanked the park ranger. He asked us if we were interested in owls, too. When we said yes, he told us to stop down the road and look in an open field surrounded by a fence.

There on a fifty-foot pole was an osprey nest. In the nest was a Great Horned Owl. Clearly a lazy but feisty owl.

We poked around the island some more. Man, there are a lot of vultures in Florida! Has the economic depression attracted them in such numbers, or is it always like this? Hardly a minute passed without us seeing either a Black or a Turkey Vulture. Often dozens at a time. Soaring, teetering, swooping, and looking for carrion. Eerie!

Our daily list had reached thirty birds in less than three hours when we decided to head out. We'd seen some great birds: a Bald Eagle (always a thrill), Northern Cardinals, Pine Warblers, Boat-tailed Grackles (better vocalizations than their Common cousins), Red-bellied Woodpeckers (pretty common), Eurasian Collared-Doves, and White Ibises to mention just a few.

On our way off the island we decided to stop at a beach on the north side of the road just before the bridge. We'd seen some gulls and waders along the shore from a distance.

The gulls included: Ring-billed, Bonaparte's, Laughing, and Great Black-backed. There were also some interesting terns. Forster's (always a special treat) and, side-by-side, a Caspian and a Royal Tern, offering a great opportunity to note the subtle differences. White crown and yellow-orange bill on the Royal, black skullcap and red-orange bill on the Caspian.

And among the gulls and terns, a special bird that, for me, also turned out to be a lifer: Black Skimmers. There were close to one hundred birds resting about ten yards offshore on land that had not been covered by the tide. One took off and flew closer. With its lower mandible skimming the smooth surface of the lagoon, it was unmistakable—even for someone who had never seen one before.

We then turned our attention to the shorebirds. Shorebirds are a challenging species for me and many people. It's often impossible to distinguish one from another, particularly when they are dressed in their winter plumage. It can be frustrating. But paying attention to behaviour near the water's edge will provide the observer with ID clues.

There were Ruddy Turnstones turning stones—always fun to see; Dunlins poking the sand and actively feeding; and Sanderlings behaving like wind-up toys.

It was a remarkable morning of birding—sharing the experience of seeing two life-birds with my friend as well as the enjoyment and challenge of finding and identifying birds in this still wild area shared with scrub-jays, rockets, and astronauts. But the best was yet to come.

On Wednesday I went back out onto Merritt Island. The day before, Charlie and I had missed the two loops north and south of Route 406. I began the south loop just past the visitor centre on Peacocks Pocket Road. No peacocks there (they wouldn't have counted anyway) but scores of herons and egrets and ibises in the shallows inside the road.

The most numerous were the ibises, both White and Glossy, because they like to hang out in groups. They're gorgeous birds in their own separate ways, the one with their pure white bodies and curved red bills and legs, and the other with their almost iridescent brown, green, and purple sheen. I searched in vain for a Scarlet Ibis or a Scarlet/White hybrid or for a vagrant White-faced Ibis. No luck there.

All three white egrets were present in considerable numbers but usually on their own: Great White with their long necks, black legs, and yellow bills; Cattle with their big, rounded heads; and, my favourites, the Snowies with their black legs and clownish yellow feet.

I was pleasantly surprised to find Roseate Spoonbills and Wood Storks present, but even happier to find the "blue herons" so close to each other in so many different spots: Little Blue, Reddish, and Tri-coloured. Reddish Herons, with their erratic, quirky fishing behaviour, jumping around and flapping their wings, were the easiest to distinguish and the most fun to watch.

My primary destination of the day, the Haulover Canal between the Indian River and the more easterly Mosquito Lagoon, was not a great birding site. I headed there to see some Manatees.

When I arrived at the Manatee Observation Deck, a dozen people were clicking away with their cameras aimed at the brown, turgid water. Most of them were trying to anticipate the time and place of the next surfacing of a couple of small, grey dolphins. There was much grumbling at near misses and not a little confusion as to whether they were actually dolphins or the sought-after manatees.

Because the water was so murky and the surfacing of the animals so unpredictable, the manatees were very difficult to spot. One briefly came up for air right below me, so close I could see its sad bulldog face. Another rolled slowly above the surface on the other side of the canal long enough for me to see a distinct scar across its dark brown back.

Gene Walz

Although manatee numbers have increased in the past year to over 5,000 individuals throughout Florida, they're still seriously endangered; scores are killed each year by fatal encounters with powerboats. So I was ecstatic to have even short glimpses of these two. They were my "species of the day."

After a mostly uneventful Thursday, I was lucky enough to get the last seat on the Friday morning bus to see "Central Florida's Specialties." Led by Wes Biggs (head of Florida Nature Tours and the person with the longest life list in Florida), Dave Goodwin (the one with the third longest list), and Adam Kent (of the Florida Fish and Wildlife Conservation Commission), we started out at 5:00 am and finished almost twelve hours later. It was a full and memorable day of birding, my birding festival "Big Day."

Highlights for me included extended, full-frame views of the endangered Red-cockaded Woodpecker, the Bachman's Sparrow, and the Brown-headed Nuthatch. Not easy birds to get, they were lifers for me.

All three birds were at the back of the Three Lakes campground. We were all more than a little nervous at first. This place is also a hunting ground and there was a guy in an orange vest with a yellow "x" stalking the area we wanted to check for birds. In fact, he turned out to be a very careful birder, not a hunter. Since none of us had orange vests, we were relieved that he was rifle-free. And yet we were not entirely comfortable. A camouflaged and over-eager hunter could blast away at us from anywhere. Oops. Thought y'all was a deer!

Nesting trees for Red-cockaded Woodpeckers all have white circles painted around them about five feet off the ground. As we walked warily past the "Gut Pit" where deer and wild pig remnants are disposed of, our guide called our attention to a painted tree fifty yards or so in front of us. As we focussed on it, Pine Warblers, catbirds, towhees, and cardinals flitted about. Then a Brown-headed Nuthatch appeared in very close range followed by the Red-cockaded Woodpecker, its red cockade barely visible but its full white face clear to everyone. Unexpectedly, Adam Kent thought he heard a Bachman's Sparrow singing; it was a bit early for them, he thought. Sure enough, one appeared on a stick halfway between our group and the woodpecker. For me, three life-birds in less than three minutes. I don't think I'll ever match that experience again!

Later, on Lake "Toho" in Kissimmee, we found a Snail Kite (another lifer for me), hundreds of Sandhill Cranes and wild turkeys, as well as many Red-shouldered Hawks, the most common raptors in the state. We also found two "uncountable" Whooping Cranes, uncountable because they were what was left of a flock introduced into Florida to provide an alternate breeding colony to the one that winters in Port Aransas, Texas. Unfortunately, most of this second flock has been virtually erased by unforeseen misfortunes—mainly bobcats and hurricanes.

Seeing Crested Caracaras is always a treat for me. With their long, yellow legs, black and white feathering, and reddish facial skin, they are unique raptors and limited in their American range. When we finished lunch at the Forever Florida Wilderness Preserve we were treated to an aerial combat between two Crested Caracaras and a Turkey Vulture that had ventured too close to their nest. The caracaras dive-bombed and chased the vulture, but it was surprisingly nimble in making its escape relatively unscathed.

Although I was exhausted when the bus finally returned to Breverd Community College (now Eastern Florida State College), the festival headquarters, I took Adam Kent's advice and went for a walk to the nearby Chain of Lakes. There I found my final lifer of the festival: a Mottled Duck. I had seen it the day before but had mistaken it for a female Mallard. If you don't look closely, you'll likely make the same mistake I did. It shows you what a good bird guide can offer.

Before I'd been invited at the last minute to Titusville, I hadn't given much thought at all to birding festivals. I'd seen their advertisements in the birding magazines, and I'd even talked to a couple of my friends who'd been enthusiastic about attending them. I guess I preferred longer trips that include more than just birding. And I preferred to be in smaller groups than the crowds that frequent festivals.

But Titusville changed my mind. I enjoyed rubbing elbows and sharing drinks with birding celebrities. It was invigorating trading stories with other birders about their great adventures and exchanging tips on where to find birds and what else to do there. (I would never have considered going birding in Columbia or Thailand if someone hadn't recommended them so highly. These places are now on my to-do list.) I should have signed up much earlier, but I still added a dozen birds, lifers, to my

North American list. And I got away from the Winnipeg winter for a week in shorts and a tee-shirt in sunny Florida.

If other birding festivals are as well-organized, full, and fruitful as Titusville's was, I may become a birding festival aficionado.

Vietnam North to South

When I went to Vietnam in February 2016, I got to the Winnipeg airport at the required time, waited in the lines to get processed, and realized after I'd checked my bags that I'd brought my Brazilian visa instead of the one for Vietnam. I wouldn't be allowed into Vietnam without it.

Panicky, I raced outside at 6:55 am. I had maybe sixty-five minutes to get to South St. Vital and back to the airport before I'd be barred from entering the plane. Nothing but Prius cabs (Prii?) outside. Arrrrgh! Not a speedy Camaro cab in sight—if there are such things. I paid a cabbie a hundred bucks to get me to and fro in an hour. I felt like I was in a weird spy movie! My two friends, John Weier and John Hays, going to Vietnam with or without me, bet against my making the flight.

On the edge of my slippery taxi seat the entire way (plastic covers like my grandma's couch), I got to my house in twenty minutes. Whew! So far so good. I tried unsuccessfully to stifle the thought that I had subconsciously sabotaged the trip.

Not much luck on the return trip. Rush hour traffic stymied us. Each second at a red traffic light felt like a Pileated Woodpecker drilling into my skull. In a dead sweat, adrenalin pumping hard enough to explode my eyeballs, I rushed into James Armstrong Richardson International Airport at 8:12 am for my 8:30 flight. The check-in attendants said I was too late. I told them that my bags were already on the plane; it would take longer to find and off-load them than for me to get through security and into my seat. They hustled me through. My friends were stunned.

As we flew to Vancouver, I remembered the premonitions I'd had about this birding trip. From the moment I hastily signed up for it, I'd had second thoughts and developed a vague, unfocussed sense of unease, apprehension. I had passed up a trip to India and wondered if I'd made the right decision. Vietnam sounded more interesting, but I wasn't fully convinced. It was the first time that I'd ever felt this way.

It was going to be a "strenuous" trip. That's what the brochure said. Would it take more stamina than I could muster, more courage? Would it be a test that I couldn't pass, an experience I wouldn't like, a country I couldn't stand? It was none of these really. What it was I couldn't quite put my finger on. When I mentioned Vietnam to friends, people's eyes widened. They too had seen the Vietnam movies and remembered the war coverage on TV. "What about the unexploded bombs?" they'd say. "Or the trip wires in the jungle?" Some even mentioned "the Commies." Would the Vietnamese people, especially in the north, be receptive to western tourists? I guess these comments contributed to my own suppressed anxiety.

Funny thing about weird premonitions: every little hint of disappointment or danger gets magnified. You think: is this going to be the moment when things go sideways into the ditch? Occasionally it gets even more dramatic: is this how it'll end? I knew that making the flight did not put a stop to my troubles.

Three weeks before my departure date I was warned by a Canadian Customs agent that my Permanent Resident Card was about to expire. She suggested to me that I would have serious difficulty re-entering Canada with an expired card. For thirty-six years I'd had a crumbling pink sheet of paper, folded to wallet-size, that I'd present at the border. My plastic replacement card lasted a mere five years, and the expiration date, which I'd never noticed, thinking it was a "permanent" Permanent Resident Card, was in fine print at the bottom of the card, overlooked unless pointed out. The agent also informed me that getting a replacement card usually took between six weeks and six months.

I decided to throw myself into the maw of government bureaucracy. I filled out the forms, included a bank note for the not insubstantial fee, and sent them express to the Immigration, Refugees, and Citizenship Canada processing centre in Sydney, Nova Scotia where, I supposed, out-of-work miners would process them. Every day I raced to my community mailbox to check return addresses. No luck. The replacement card did not arrive by my departure date.

Decision time. Do I wait for the card, buy a new ticket at that time, and join the tour late? No, it could arrive five months after the trip was over. Do I cancel the entire trip, forfeit the big bucks I'd already spent, and erase all those spooky premonitions? No, I decided to worry about my return when the time came, get on a plane, and go. Risk-taking can be bracing!

For the first time ever, this birding trip was going to begin in Hanoi and head south. Tours in the opposite direction had ended anti-climactically; birds were few and far between in the north, and the weather was chillier. The two Johns and I arrived three days before the official tour was to commence and the weather was fine. Just how many of the 850 species of birds of Vietnam could we find?

Leaving our hotel on our first morning, we were immediately struck by the birdsong—lots of it—in that crowded, noisy, urban neighborhood reeking with the smell of several million motorbikes. Then we discovered that all the birdsongs were coming from caged birds. Mostly jittery Red-whiskered Bulbuls and white-eyes in tiny wooden cages. Bulbuls predominated because of their bubbly, insistent, and incessant singing. It was truly depressing, a very bad sign. On our first bird walk in Hanoi, we saw more caged birds than free ones.

Our hotel was in the middle of the quaint old quarter of Hanoi, a place of short, very narrow streets lined with small shops devoted to different bits of merchandise. Fish street, metal goods street, flower street, toy street, tools street, etc. The sidewalks were clogged with parked motorbikes. We had to walk in the streets—which were clogged with motorbikes driven intently by people of all ages wearing colourful surgical masks to combat the pollution. Traffic followed the North American pattern except for outriders who felt that the space closest to the sidewalks was for motorbikes travelling in the opposite direction. We had to constantly look over our shoulders for bikes that could take us out from behind. Every walk was a bit risky. My mind kept turning to irony. Headline: Birder offed by Vietnamese motorbike carrying an elephant-sized cargo of flowers.

Wanting something calmer and birdier, we headed for an island in the Red River outside the centre of the city. We'd heard it had some good birds.

To get there, we had to cross a rickety, old iron bridge with narrow pedestrian walkways on each side, two lanes of traffic, and a railroad track. The bridge was probably a kilometre long. During what the Vietnamese call "the American War" (as opposed to the French and Japanese Wars), American prisoners were lined up on the bridge so that it wouldn't be bombed. Somebody should bomb it now. Walking it was a scary experience. Many of the cement slabs on the sidewalks wobbled in their metal struts when you stepped on them. We felt as if we could plunge forty feet to our deaths at any minute. When a train chugged by, it seemed like the entire structure was about to collapse. More ironic headlines flashed through my brain.

Once on the island, we didn't see as many birds as we'd hoped due to an obstacle that kept the count down. As we came out of a grove of trees and rounded the corner on a muddy path, we came upon a meadow with a water buffalo grazing in the centre. He glared at us and started to charge. Ironic headline: Birder gored and stomped by a water buffalo? Luckily, it was tethered by a huge metal ring through its nostrils. Its rope kept it from reaching us but would have allowed it to get to us if we followed the path. We turned back. Still, we recorded fifteen species for the day, seven lifers for me. Not bad.

Our first official day of birding took us on a long bus ride along a smooth, modern, four-lane divided highway with rice paddies all along the way. They were being worked by hand; some of them had small cemeteries with oddly shaped tombstones in the middle of them. At our destination, Cuc Phuong National Park, we learned the basic realities of tropical birding. It's a lot like war—without the killing. Hours of empty boredom and fruitless searching followed by minutes of frantic action and panic. You hear more birds than you see, and others in the group see more birds than you do because of their positioning near the bird guide. The foliage is so thick, the openings so narrow, and the birds so flitty and wary that seeing them is more than a challenge. It was a frustrating introduction.

We really had to earn our birds. At one point we all struggled up a path equivalent to a twenty-three storey building in search of a bird we didn't find. Still, I managed to spot six of the ten target birds for the park, several with fabulous names: Ratchet-tailed Treepie (tree-pie like magpie, not tree-pee), Rufous-tailed Fulvetta (not Velveeta), Limestone Wren-Babbler, and Fujian Niltava. Bird-of-the-park for me was a Bar-bellied Pitta, a secretive ground bird with a stumpy tail, lime green head and back, yellow underparts with brown barring, and a blue rump. It's so big and brightly coloured you'd think it would be easy to spot—not so. A wonderful bird.

Just before leaving Cuc Phuong we paid a visit to the Primate Rescue Center where we saw fifteen different species of the area's most endangered primates, mostly gibbons and langurs. We were able to see some wild langurs at our next stop, Van Long Wetland Nature Reserve. Two each in very narrow, shallow, and tippy boats, we were poled around the marshland to the backside of a mountain where Delacour's langurs roamed the cliffs. Only 200 of these critically endangered monkeys remain. We saw six of the black and white langurs, their six-foot-long tails and fuzzy hairdos clear even at a distance. As we watched, a Black Eagle soared overhead. The marshland produced the only ducks of the trip, Garganeys, and most of the marshbirds: Common Moorhens, Purple Swamphens, White-browed Crakes, and the fantastic Pheasant-tailed Jacana with its enormous silver feet, white head and wings, brown and black body, and yellow hindneck that resembles an odd mullet. Swinging around quickly to spot birds in flight threatened to capsize the boats; so, not tempting fate, I missed the Yellow Bittern that others saw. Safety first.

After Van Long, we headed for Tam Dao, a former French hill station, now a thriving tourist town because its cool, mountain temperatures contrast so nicely with Vietnam's hot, humid climate. Our new, modern hotel had marble throughout but no heat. And the mattresses were as hard as granite; a hammer and chisel wouldn't take a chip out of them. Cuc Phuong's mattresses were hard too, but they provided two duvets and I used one for a mattress pad. Here there was only one duvet. Is this how it'll end? Frozen to death on a ready-made slab?

A storefront restaurant across from the hotel had the usual red children's chairs and tables for all its customers—about a foot off the ground. In front was the five-by-eight-foot table with the daily choice of meat products set out from opening to closing time. There was the entire side of a hog, a couple of skinned squirrels, some piglets, a porcupine with some quills still on it (built-in toothpicks?), and an unplucked Silver Pheasant. One of our group tried to take a photo but she was chased away as some of the offerings were illegal. We did not eat there.

Birding around Tam Dao was tough. We searched desperately along a motorbike trail that led, unbeknownst to us, to a popular teenage gathering spot. We had to constantly make way for the speedy bikes, sometimes barely. Is this how it'll end? Clipped by a dirtbike driver on a cell phone? After a while, saying "xin chao" (sin-chow: hello) to them lost its charm.

The birding there was a disappointment; long, arduous walks with only five of fifteen possible target birds spotted. One morning, we heard a Slaty-bellied Tesia noisily singing in a weedy embankment only four feet away from us. This bird, the size of a mouse with a grey belly and olive back, eluded everyone but me. After an hour search, I caught a glimpse of it as it scampered upright past an opening right opposite me. Everyone else had to list it as "Heard Only."

Highlights were an aptly named Red-billed Blue Magpie and several delightful Short-tailed Parrotbills, tiny rufous-headed birds with grey backs, white underparts, and over-sized, yellow, parrot-shaped bills.

After Tam Dao we bussed back to Hanoi, flew south to Hue, and took a waiting bus to another national park, Bach Ma. Bach Ma means "white horse" in Vietnamese. We quickly discovered why: the park is usually in the clouds which resemble a giant white horse. Those (all!) of us hoping for a reprieve from the cold of Tam Dao were quickly disillusioned. Bach Ma was cold, rainy, and grey.

Most of us had to traverse a rocky, puddle-filled path to get to our rooms. They were in an ancient, leaky building that had seen better days, probably six or seven decades prior to our arrival. It was clear that the floors had been swabbed with disinfectant moments before our arrival. They hadn't dried by the time we left. Electricity was limited to three hours per day around mealtimes. There was no heat; it was so cold that most of us slept fully clothed, listening to the rodents having a good time slopping around in the disinfectant under our beds. We didn't dare shower in the cold darkness in the morning. At breakfast, there was a campfire in the middle of the dining room. The washroom contained a pail. Sartre was wrong. Hell isn't other people; it's Bach Ma. Headline: Frigid, unwashed birders die of smoke inhalation in Vietnamese dining room.

Fortunately, we were treated to close-up views of a very cooperative target bird—an Indochinese Wren-Babbler formerly called a Short-tailed Scimitar Babbler, which was a more descriptive name because of its long, curved bill and short tail. But its the size and colour of a wren and sings like one so the name change wasn't entirely arbitrary as some seem to be. We also had a great sighting of a male Silver Pheasant walking slowly across the road, its peacock size and silver back, wings, and long tail brilliantly unmistakable.

We all needed a break. Luckily, we got one back in Hue, one of the cities at the centre of the Vietnam War. For lunch we ate in the leafy courtyard of the fantastic Hotel Saigon Morin, a marvellous example of French Colonial architecture. Charlie Chaplin and Paulette Goddard stopped here in 1932; their photo is in a wonderful gallery. Another photo shows US marines in foxholes dug right outside the entrance. Now gloriously restored, it was a welcome recovery from Bach Ma.

So too was an afternoon tour of the old Imperial City. It seemed bigger and more ornate (and decadent) than the Forbidden City in Beijing, Next door is an outdoor war-remnants museum the size of a couple of football fields. Jet fighters, various helicopters, tanks, anti-aircraft guns, jeeps, and other pieces of abandoned or captured US military equipment are on display there. It was an all-too-eerie reminder of the war that I had barely missed. I wonder if there were any soldiers who birded between battles, who returned from the war with Vietnam bird lists.

From Hue we travelled to Phong Nha-Ke Bang National Park. Here, we boarded sampans and were poled downriver and into Son Doong cave, probably the world's largest cavern. It's the biggest space I've ever been in, its size and odd formations truly awe-inspiring. We didn't get much birding done, on the river or inside the cave, but by the end of the day, we'd gotten good looks at what our guide called "the endemic and charismatic Sooty Babbler"—small and sooty—and "the almost mythical Red-collared Woodpecker"—a very tough-to-find, large, olive-green bird with a red head and upper breast. It led us on a merry chase, zipping behind us from one side of a road to the other, from one impenetrable grove to an even denser one. Irony: Birder dies of whiplash.

Our next day was a long travel day. Days like this can make you wish you were struggling mightily up and down some intimidating mountain trail, chasing unforgettable or un-get-able birds. Typical in some ways—up in the dark for a quick breakfast and early bird walk—it was mostly a day of cramped, bird-free tedium. Even a special beach stop to find, successfully, the recently discovered White-faced Plover was marred by the debris that covered its marvellous white sandy beach environment. Vietnam is a beautiful country but the carelessly strewn garbage—everywhere—scars the soul.

Another bus ride took us to Lo Xo Pass where a long walk in the woods produced our target bird for the day, the recently discovered but otherwise unremarkable Black-crowned Barwing. On to the newly developed town of Mang Den, where we trudged the nearby logging roads to catch a glimpse of the Chestnut-eared Laughingthrush, only discovered in 1999. We also found its cousin the Black-hooded Laughingthrush; these elusive birds do sound as if they're laughing at you as they flit almost undetected through the thick foliage.

Too far from our home base, we had lunch at a roadside shack with corrugated tin walls and roof supported by tree branches. We had to squat down onto those plastic kiddie chairs again; they were uncomfortable but out of the intense heat of the sun, providing some much needed shade. For lunch we had the typical Pho, various greens (perhaps morning glory) and small, indecipherable pieces of meat in a clear broth. Untypical was the source of the broth: a large 500 gallon drum of rainwater, boiled of course. None of us got sick, but I think we all imagined a headline: Ten birders and two guides die of food poisoning.

Our reward: some great birds after lunch, including self-explanatory Pale Blue Flycatchers, Maroon Orioles, Stripe-breasted Woodpeckers, Grey-crowned Tits, and Yellow-billed Nuthatches, as well as Blue-winged Minla (or Siva, names often change here), a cute, slim, white-bellied bird with a brown back and, surprise, blue wing fringes.

A plane ride, a pokey bus trip through traffic-clogged Ho Chi Minh City (HCMC), and a short ferry ride brought us to Cat Tien National Park for three hot, hot days in a lowland tropical forest. Craig Robson, the writer of *A Field Guide to the Birds of South-East Asia* which we all were using, was already at the park. We were happy to see him until we learned that he had commandeered all of the good safari vehicles. We were stuck with the banged up pick-up trucks with plank seating in the beds to get us to and from our birding sites. I pulled a muscle on one of the bumpier rides and hobbled around painfully for the rest of the trip. If you were lucky enough to get in the lead vehicle, you were bumped around but otherwise okay; if you got the following vehicle, you ate dust. We all took turns eating dust. Headline: Birders die of dust poisoning.

We spent three and a half days at Cat Tien, serenaded early every morning by the mournful whistles of a family of buff-cheeked gibbons high in the trees just opposite our cabins. A routine was established the first day: up at 4:45 am or so, a quick breakfast, a bumpy ride, long walks 'til noon or so, lunch, a brief respite (for a change of sweat-soaked clothes), a second ride, more long walks 'til 7:00 pm, a quick shower, the compilation of the day's birds, dinner, and socializing, emailing, or reading—usually a preparatory scan of the bird guide for the next day's outing. Not too much different from previous stops, but by this point, most of us were knackered by mid-morning.

Our main target bird for Cat Tien was the endemic Germaine's Peacock Pheasant. We spent hours and hours searching for it to no avail. That's how birding goes sometimes.

As compensation, we did have clear views of Great Hornbills and lots of galliformes: both Scaly-breasted and Orange-necked Partridges, some Red Junglefowl (like spectacular farm roosters), stunning Green Peafowl (like our zoo's peacocks but emerald green), and, in our guide's words, "the superlative-defying Siamese Fireback," a peacock-sized groundbird with a grey body fading to purplish-black underneath, a large, green-black tail with a fiery patch on the rump, a red face, and a dainty top-knot.

We also notched ten different kinds of woodpeckers, including the scarce Pale-headed, plus a Blue-rumped Pitta, a Siberian Blue Robin, and a Tickell's Blue Flycatcher when we thought we'd seen everything. Red-breasted Parakeets entertained us with fly-overs during the day, followed by Great-eared Nightjars just after dusk.

Our final destination was Da Lat, another temperate resort city situated on top of a plateau. Home to over 200,000 people and probably as many motorbikes, Da Lat, remarkably, has no traffic lights or stop signs. Our hotel, modern and comfortable in almost every way, was called

Dreams but produced nightmares; it had no elevator. We had to clamber up three or four flights of stairs after every exhausting bird search. Hard on hearts, death on arthritic knees, especially at the end of a tour!

To make matters worse, half of our number started to get sick with a vicious bug that emptied us out, top and bottom. I was the only one of the stricken five who didn't spend at least a day in bed, missing the great birding opportunities that this Important Endemic Birding Area provided.

The lack of elevators was especially painful after a day at Lang Bian Mountain. Jeeps took us to a lofty drop-off point. As we exited, our guide heard a scarce Vietnamese Cutia singing about one hundred metres farther up. We had to scramble up a rocky, fifty degree slope covered with pine needles to see it then risk warbler-neck or toppling over backwards to find it at the very top of the pine trees. A decorator's combination of a slate-blue crown with a thick black face, chestnut back and rump, and white underparts with black barring, the bird was worth the effort. But what an effort to start the day!

Then we trudged higher, on broken, rocky terrain through briars and thick tangles in search of the almost-impossible-to-find Collared Laughingthrushes. It probably took an hour to get a good look at them after we first heard them and caught fleeting glimpses. But what a sight! With black hoods, silvery ear patches, muted gray-gold backs, and bright orange bellies and collars, they were worth the effort. We spent almost as much time trying to catch sight of a Grey-bellied Tesia, a small, mousy forest-floor denizen with a loud, almost ventriloquist's call. It's there. No, it's there. Its call is coming from right over there. No, it isn't. Our silent, crouching patience finally paid off. We caught a long glimpse of the Tesia as skittered across an opening, enough of a glimpse to include it as one of the "birds of the day."

Ta Nung Valley was hardly any easier, though for this spot, we descended down a long, steep hill in the morning and struggled up at noon, and then repeated it. Our highlight birds here were some Orange-breasted Laughingthrushes who weren't where they were supposed to be and some Grey-crowned Crocias, oriole-sized birds that almost duplicate the markings of the Cutias.

My last night in Da Lat was agony. I caught the virus that the four others had suffered through earlier. Severe cramps and the attendant

GI track evacuations. Thus, I surmised, were the pre-trip premonitions finally realized. I felt like death barely warmed over. No headlines, just a quiet burial in a good birding spot, please.

On our way from Da Lat back to HCMC on our final day, we made a brief stop at Datanla Waterfall. I raced to the park's washroom four times in an hour but still managed to see some of the best birds of the trip: Orange-headed Thrushes, a spectacular Red-headed Trogon, a White-throated Rock Thrush, a Eurasian Jay, and, to cap it all off, another Cutia.

I was starved and wasted by the time we got to our posh hotel in HCMC. Birding now done, I turned my full attention to a more urgent problem—re-entering into Canada. I had two days to get an emergency Permanent Resident Card. Get one, and I could stop worrying. Get denied, and, as I was warned, I could be detained at the airport, or at the Seoul airport for my connecting flight, or denied entry in Vancouver. The irony was clear. All my pre-trip anxieties about going to Vietnam were now focussed on getting out of Vietnam.

After a hasty breakfast and heart-felt farewells to the non-Winnipeg birders, I headed to the Canadian visa application office. At the door, I was given a number; inside, I took a seat with twenty-four Vietnamese applicants. The wait was excruciating. I considered alternate strategies. Since my visa expired the day after I was supposed to leave, I was going to have to get out of HCMC quickly. My plan: buy a new ticket, fly anywhere, get a connection to some US border city, and figure things out there. Sneaking across the border like a drug dealer was, I confess, one idea.

When my turn finally came, a Vietnamese lad with perfect British English heard my pleas. I'd already had passport photos taken and filled out the forms. He told me there was little hope; applications took a month to six weeks in his experience. He copied and faxed my application anyway, along with my passport and Vietnamese visa. I was now paperless in HCMC where even a hotel demanded passports and visas to register and I hadn't yet registered in our new, cheaper hotel.

The hotel clerk reluctantly let me register without the proper credentials. In my room, I called the Canadian Consulate. The automatic answering service required me to press one. Every time I did, I got the hotel clerk. It took me four frustrating calls to realize my mistake. I went

133

down and called from her phone. A woman at the consulate told me that they could surely help. I didn't take her name. When I got to the consulate, the people there told me that they could not help at all.

I left the consulate angry and bewildered. Wandering down the street, I was offered a ride by a motorbike cabbie. The cost was reasonable: thirty Dong, about a buck and a half Canadian. With a backpack slung over my right shoulder and a sheaf of documents in my left hand, I hopped on. Our guide had told us there were six million motorbikes and scooters in HCMC. They all seemed to converge on us in a Darwinian nightmare, me with no helmet, holding onto the seat with one hand, and trying not to scrape my knees on adjoining bikes, trucks, buses, and cars, yet not squeezing them into the driver.

Unscathed and back in my hotel room, I spent the rest of the day waiting for a phone call and planning for the worst. Very little sleep that night, if any.

The next morning, I went back to the visa application office. More waiting. When I got to my agent, I re-emphasized that I needed things resolved by closing time that afternoon, 3:30 pm. My plane left before they opened the next morning. He sent a fax somewhere saying I needed my passport and visa back that day. I walked home, not willing to risk suicide-by-motorbike again. I sat nervously in my hotel room for the rest of the day. My two friends went birding and touring.

At 2:50 pm I got a call from the consulate: come and get your papers. Which ones? They didn't say. John Hays and I rushed to the consulate. A young guy was there waiting to replace a lost Canadian passport. We commiserated. I waited behind him. The people who were rude and unhelpful the day before now smiled at me. I was given an envelope. Inside were my passport and visa. I opened the passport. Pasted on page 12 was a temporary Permanent Resident Card. Whew! At 3:10 I was free to go—with only twenty minutes to spare.

I stashed my papers at the hotel and decided to head to the zoo where my friends had earlier seen some interesting birds—not in cages but on the well-forested grounds. At the zoo and on the way, I added seven new birds for the trip, including Little Cormorant, Black-headed Ibis, twelve Painted Storks, and nine Lesser Adjutants—huge, stork-like birds with black backs and white bellies. Adjutants = aides. Great symbolism there for my final birds of the trip.

I took another motorbike cab back to the hotel. It was rush hour and even scarier. Risky, I know, but I felt exhilarated and invulnerable. As we raced to a corner, my right knee scraped a strip of dirt off the bus next to me. The last close call of many.

That night, I contemplated all the ups and downs of the trip. I felt like a warbler must feel after a very tough migration. Completely spent.

Was it worth the aggravation? Absolutely! The birding was difficult, but the rewards were many. We tallied over 300 species of birds, many of them endemics that I'd never get a chance to see again. 280 of them or so were lifers for me, birds I'd never seen before. The animals—langurs and gibbons, the deer, and even the many squirrels—were a gratifying bonus.

More broadly, Vietnam was, of all the countries I've visited, the most unique. You know you're in a special place when you see a man safely leading a water buffalo across an eight lane divided highway with no traffic lights at rush hour. Or people in a supposedly Catholic country burning fake money on curbsides to appeal to the gods for the real thing.

Vietnam's combination of old and new, modern and ancient, urban and rural, rich and poor is striking. The people are friendly and helpful, seeming to bear no grudge at all for past Western aggression and its destructiveness. It was amusing to sample their food, from Vietnamese caphe (coffee with an egg yolk, condensed milk, and sugar) to Ba Ba Ba (333, their beer), to porcupine meat (terrible!), and to their fresh, un-modified vegetables and fruit (especially their watermelon, the sweetest, tastiest treat I've had since I was young). I only wish they'd pick up their garbage.

Add new last paragraph. As for the weird premonitions I had before I left, I guess I now have to worry—now that I'm older—that I may have discovered my inner "worry wart." I'll have to stifle this latent creature. Despite all the troubles I endured in Vietnam, I lived through it. No permanent bruises. No poisonous snake bites. No stints in jail or in customs detention. And some great birds and amusing stories. "Don't worry, be happy." It's now one of my favourite songs.

My Birding Bruises

About fifteen years ago at a Christmas Bird Count, I was bitten by a Doberman pinscher. The temperature was well below zero Fahrenheit and my friend Jerry was leading a silent group of birders across his deck, each of us intently searching for an over-wintering and thus aptly named Mourning Dove. Suddenly, Jerry's Doberman sneaked up behind us and, without warning, bit me on the butt.

Twelve cheeks to select from and the dog chose my right one. (If he'd chosen the left, he'd have pinsched my wallet.) He broke the skin, right through my ski pants, jeans, and insulated underwear. Startled, I let out a yelp that scared every bird clean out of the count area. We never did find the Mourning Dove, I remained in mourning, and Jerry became my ex-friend until he got rid of the dog.

Of course, the story made the rounds, and I became perhaps the second-most notorious person to be bitten on the butt. David Howells Fleay (after whom the Fleay's barred frog is named) was nipped on the buttocks by a Tasmanian tiger. It just happened to be the last remaining one in the world, and Fleay was photographing it in the Hobart Zoo. He bragged about his scar for the rest of his life. I don't.

It wasn't the first or the last time I limped home, bruised and/or battered, after a day of birding. When I was a kid, I fell out of a tree while trying to retrieve an abandoned vireo's nest. I broke the branch the nest was on and then a couple of pretty useful (when unbroken) bones. Some refer to this early episode of my birding life as "One Cuckoo Fell Out of the Vireo's Nest."

I've also had several sprains and strains, plus welts and bruises of every colour and description. Maybe I should have kept a life list of injuries as well as one for the birds.

The list would include other kinds of bites besides the Doberman's. Nasty bites from Kamikaze bees. From cartoon-sized black flies. From hornets with lasers instead of stingers. From dark, noisy battalions of mosquitoes in Churchill, Manitoba—mosquitoes that ate bug repellant for breakfast and used what seemed to be computer-assisted guidance systems, as eerily effective as smart bombs, to find exposed flesh.

In Brazil, nobody told me that the ticks there are as small as freckles until the first of over seventy festering, itchy welts sprang up on my body in private, sweaty places. It took almost a month for the last one to disappear. And the chiggers! Who knew they could penetrate your wool socks and cover your feet with bites—including between your toes?! Almost drove me crazy.

I've somehow managed to incur almost as many injuries from birding as I did from more than fifty years of full contact sports such as football, hockey, and basketball. It all makes me wonder sometimes whether I've settled into the wrong pastime.

My worst encounter almost proved deadly. It was a simple outing to an eastern Manitoba wilderness area. My friend Andy and I took the morning off to look for Golden-winged Warblers and Yellow-bellied Flycatchers. (If I were superstitious, I'd say that you should never chase after two hyphenated birds at once.) We found our warbler easily enough, sitting near the top of an ash tree. Buzzy song, black cheeks, yellow wing bars. Check. Then we saw a Northern Parula and a Nashville Warbler. Good bonus birds.

But there were no Yellow-bellied Flycatchers to be found. We searched all the black spruce bogs to no avail. Whenever we saw even a single black spruce, we stopped, got out of Andy's toy pickup truck, and looked around. We played a tape and listened for a response. No luck. Then we got back into the truck and moved on.

After a while, our search became a comic routine. Stop the truck. Clamber out. Play the tape. Listen. Look around. Get back in. Bang your elbow. Bump your head. Scrape your shin. Wrestle with the dad-blasted seat belts. No, forget about the dad-blasted seat belts! Move on. Let the car's bleeping mother-in-law warning system beep away!

Bad idea.

As we rounded a banked turn on a narrow gravel road, I thought I caught something out of the corner of my eye. Andy did too. We both looked up. In a flash, the pickup strayed six inches from the beaten track and hit the soft gravel at the side of the road, and then a slight washout.

Before we could do anything, we careened off the road, hurtling down a twenty-foot embankment. We were bounced around the cab of the pickup like dice in a tumbler, our binoculars, bird guides, scopes, and tripods menacing us about the head and shoulders. Tree branches lashed us through the open windows.

Despite the steep incline, the rocks, and the tree trunks, somehow the pickup didn't flip over. It should have, but Andy's coolness and the great god of birding kept the truck upright. If it had flipped, we'd have ended up in two feet of cold snowmelt, upside down, hidden from the rarely used road, and probably seriously injured, or worse. As it was, we were badly shaken and pretty banged up. But we would live to bird another day.

I wish I could tell you that we heard a Yellow-bellied Flycatcher as we waited (for four hours) for a tow truck to arrive and winch the truck out of the deep ditch. About all I heard was Andy's repeated refrain: "Sam's gonna kill me!"

Sam (actually Sandra, his wife) did not live up to this dire prediction, but she has become decidedly more insistent with her warning, "If you bird, don't drive. If you drive, don't bird." Excellent advice.

All I can add are the immortal words of a former television cop: "Be careful out there." Birding isn't as tame as you might think. The life list you save may be your own.

Looking for Potoos
A Deadly Encounter

P otoos are members of the nightjar or frogmouth family (*Nyctibius*). They're weird-looking birds. Shaped like owls, they sit erect like owls, and they hunt at night like most owls. But they have wide, thin beaks, similar to a nighthawk. They look like an odd cross between an owl, a frog, and a tree stump.

Because they're so well-camouflaged and hunt at night from broken-off tree trunks and branches about four to five metres off the ground, they are difficult to find. They are at the top of most birders' "must-see" lists in Central and South America.

Led by our guide Domingo and his assistant Felix, John Weier and I set out at dusk one drizzly evening from Sani Lodge in the Amazonian section of Ecuador. It was about 5:30 pm; the sun sets in the area at 6:15 or so every day of the year.

We were all looking up for the potoos. We should have been looking down, too.

All of a sudden, Domingo, who was leading our group of five searchers, jumped sideways and backwards right into me. I staggered back into the next guy, figuring we were all going to topple over like dominoes. At first it was weirdly funny.

Then: "Essnake," said Domingo, by way of explanation.

On the path, four feet from my leg, was a thick, brown snake with beige markings and a triangle-shaped head. I'd seen one of these vipers years before in Costa Rica but from considerably further away. It was a fer-de-lance (*Bothrops atrox*), one of the deadliest vipers in the tropics. A deadly, game-over snake. It can strike a person its body length away.

We all backed away very slowly. Although they are well-known for being aggressive, this one did not strike again.

We eyed it for a couple of moments, waiting to see whether it would slither away. It didn't. So Felix cut a new path through the jungle with his machete and we proceeded with our hunt. We looked both up at the trees for potoos and down at the path for snakes.

After much searching, Domingo finally spotted a Rufous Potoo (*Nyctibius bracteatus*). Because it wasn't roosting in its usual spot, it took us much longer to find it. And it was perfectly disguised—sitting on the top of a rotting, broken-off tree trunk like an extension of that trunk. It was on a nest, a simple hollow in the top of the trunk.

On the way back to the lodge, Domingo used his spotlight to illuminate the path, especially where the fer-de-lance had been. He walked very warily. We all did. Luckily, the snake was gone. Maybe Felix had dispatched of it with his machete.

Before we got to the lodge, we heard and then spotted a second potoo, a Common Potoo (*Nyctibius griseus*). Plus a Tropical Screech-Owl (*Megascops choliba*) and we heard but couldn't see a Tawny-bellied Screech-Owl (*Megascops watsonii*). Our search for it was at best half-hearted. It was pitch-dark now, and the fer-de-lance had gotten inside all of our heads.

At our nightly tally, we noted that the most numerous birds of the day were TVs and BVs—Turkey Vultures and Black Vultures. Far too ironic and ominous!

Later, Domingo admitted he hadn't seen the fer-de-lance until it sprang at him and was inches from his leg. He recognized it in mid-strike from the whiteness inside its mouth. It had missed him by inches, me by a foot or so. Whew!

When pressed, he said that no one among his people had died from a fer-de-lance bite in about four years. There was anti-venom at the lodge.

Three lifers and one huge scare. Ah, jungle birding! Adventure birding at its best.

Scary Surprise on an
Amazonian Birding Tower

I wasn't the least bit afraid of heights when I was young. I remember standing on the third step from the top of a thirty-foot extension ladder to paint the peak of our three-storey house one summer. No problem.

I guess I've gotten smarter over the years. Heights now make me pretty nervous. I hire a younger guy each fall to clean out my second-storey gutters.

When I decided to go to Ecuador, I knew I was going to have to deal with my old-age acrophobia. Getting up into the canopy of the trees or above it via birding towers is crucial for spotting tropical birds. I promised myself I'd go as high up as it took.

At the Sani Lodge on the Napo River in Ecuadorian Amazonia I got my chance to test my resolve. Sani Lodge was built by an oil company. They wanted the rights to explore for oil on the local people's land. The oil company was willing to pay dearly for the privilege, and promised more millions should they discover oil. The tribe asked them to finance the building of a modern but rustic-looking nature lodge; this included a steel birding tower. The facilities have provided a steady source of employment and money for the Sani community, though the oil company never did discover oil. (Years later the company asked to explore with newer, more sophisticated technologies. The tribe turned them down flat.)

Early on the morning of our second day at the lodge, we hiked out to the green steel tower. It's about ten or twelve storeys high. When we got to the base, I deliberately didn't calculate the height or even look up to see how tall it was. I knew it would be a challenge. Tough on the knees, tough on the psyche.

To keep myself from bailing out, I deliberately went first. Up a skeletal, open structure, more like a series of ladders than staircases. Steep, wet, meshy, see-through steps and minimal leadpipe rails made it an added challenge. I put a steely grip on both handrails and willed myself up.

About two-thirds of the way up the tower, I had to stop and catch my breath in the middle of a stairway. As I stood there looking straight ahead, neither up nor down nor sideways, I kept my rigid grip on the pipe-rails with both hands. Suddenly, our guide Domingo ducked under my right arm and went ahead.

Within seconds he touched my arm from above with his walking stick. I was concentrating so hard, I almost jumped out of my skin. "Essnake," he whispered.

Ahead, in a corner of the next landing, was an eight-inch coil of lime green—a diamond-headed snake. If I'd gone three or four steps farther, I'd have been staring right into its small, beady eyes. When I think about it, I envision myself becoming a Tex Avery cartoon character: my eyes popping out of my skull, my limbs extended, and my body fragmenting into uncountable pieces.

The others crept up behind me to get a good look. We all gulped. Audibly. Then Domingo's silent gestures indicated we were going up. I guess he didn't prod the snake off the tower with his walking stick because he feared pushing it down on us.

Continue up or head back down? I knew if I let others go ahead of me, I might decide to go back to the lodge.

With instructions from Domingo, I turned sideways, grabbed the right "handrail,"—a thin lead pipe—behind me with both hands, and cautiously inched past the snake. It eyed me but never moved.

My knees were jelly when I got to the top of the tower. A twelve-foot bridge was all that separated me from the wooden platform at the top of a giant kapok tree. I grabbed the rails with both hands, closed my eyes, and crossed it.

Once on the platform, I opened my eyes and reached for a wooden support nailed to a tree limb. Domingo grabbed my arm. "Bulleet ant," he said, pointing to a huge ant about an inch and a half long.

I was getting used to his exaggerated accent. "Bullet ant?"

"Eef eet bites you, eet feels like you heet by a bullet." All of his accent wasn't amusing anymore. I gulped hard.

It took me a while to get my equilibrium. Using binoculars at this height just aggravated my acrophobia.

The first bird I saw? A Blackpoll Warbler. All I could think was: Man, I can see this in my own Canadian backyard at a much lower level! All this aggravation for a Blackpoll Warbler?! Then the Kiskadees and the Tropical Kingbirds arrived—two species also found in North American.

But we did have a productive morning in the canopy. Lots of parrots and macaws, toucans and aracaris, an Ornate Hawk-eagle, and many kinds of brilliantly coloured tanagers to name just a few. The climb was sure worth it. But going down was going to be no easier.

In fact, it was scarier. I knew that the snake was still there because my friend John Weier, afflicted by the Amazonian touristas, had been up and down the steps four times during the day. Much braver than me, he'd practically worn out his Adam's apple gulping as he passed the snake!

Making matters worse, my solution to acrophobia (don't look down!) was gone. I couldn't help but look down. I slithered past the snake and hurried on jelly knees to the bottom.

Back at the lodge we discovered that the snake was a deadly Amazonian palm viper, sometimes called a two-striped forest pit-viper (*Bothriechys bilineate*). These snakes usually hang out in trees. No one at the lodge had ever seen one on the tower before.

It would have to pick my day on the tower as its first!

Big Jags and Bad Drivers

So, we're sitting on two rough wooden benches in the open box of a small pick-up truck. Four of us—Rudolf Koes, Peter Taylor, Brad Carey, and me—bouncing in the dark along rutted trails in southwest Brazil. We're in the Pantanal, a tropical wetland near the Bolivia-Paraguay border, and we're on our nightly safari.

Our guide, Kefany, is young and perky, much younger than any other guide I've ever met. But she is very knowledgeable. She's strapped into a metal seat mounted above the right front bumper of the pick-up. She's got a powerful searchlight and she's scanning right and left, up and down, into the impenetrable jungle darkness, trying to spot some night critters. Owls and potoos and flying whatnots.

The truck is painted orange with black and white splotches in an imitation jaguar pattern. It's not a great disguise. Every animal in the area knows it's a truck. Most of the local animals are inured to its noisy presence, especially jaguars, the most wary and secretive of the big cats.

That's what we're hoping to see. We'd already met up with an ocelot. We were on a small bridge and it was right below us, not six feet away. Twice the size of a house cat, it was clearly not domestic. Even lying prone by the river, casually drinking, it wordlessly said, "Don't mess with me!"

Kefany had not seen a jaguar in a month and the head of the jaguar recovery program at the Caiman Ecological Refuge had not seen one for the first two weeks he was here, and seen only thirty or so in six months. Even the jaguar with a radio collar had eluded him. But he said that a capybara corpse had been found, probably killed by a jag the night before, and that this might be a good place to watch and wait.

Brazil is the birdiest country in the world, or one of the birdiest. It's on most serious birders' itineraries as *the* place to go. Most of them head for the infamous Amazon. We chose the Pantanal, a wetland during the rainy season but now dried up. It promised more than 650 different species of birds. We were there to find as many of them as we could in a week.

One hundred metres from the front steps of the Baiazinha Lodge where we were staying, a pair of Hyacinth Macaws was nesting. The largest of the macaws and among the rarest (and the noisiest!), these magnificent, long-tailed, deep-blue birds had been an inspiration for us every morning as we set out at dawn for our daily bird search.

The macaws weren't the only spectacular birds we'd seen in the Pantanal. Jabiru Storks, another iconic bird of the area, were a constant presence. With their thick, storky bills, black and white bodies, and raspberry-red necks, they captured our attention whenever we came upon them, even in their slow, lumbering flights.

Overall, we would spot more than 200 species of birds—not bad for a week during dry season. But the highlight of our stay was not the birds. It was the animals we encountered.

The Caiman Ecological Refuge is trying to model itself on the great African safari lodges. Just as lodges in Kenya and Tanzania advertise "the big five" game animals (lion, hippo, cheetah, rhinoceros, and cape buffalo or some variant, including elephant or wildebeest), The Refuge has its own version: jaguar (third largest big cat in the world after tiger and lion), tapir (as big as a cow), giant anteater (over six feet from nose to tail), capybara (largest rodent in the world), and red deer (largest deer in South America). We didn't care all that much about the others—we wanted a jag. The other four are not quite in the same league as the "charismatic mega-fauna" of Africa.

We had begun staking out the capybara corpse just after nightfall (6 pm). Within a half hour another safari vehicle pulls up next to us on the right. A small pond is directly in front of us about twenty metres away. Across the pond is a low grassy hill with the jungle right behind. It takes a while for our eyes to adjust to the dark. There is no dusk in the jungle.

It's like somebody hit the off switch. One minute it's day and the next it's the dead of night.

After ten minutes of restless anticipation, a shape emerges from the bushes; the spotlights flash on and catch it in their powerful beams. A jag. We all gasp. It is much bigger than I'd ever imagined.

We are at most twenty-five metres away and gape in amazement. Its eyes glow a menacing red, but it does not flinch from the spotlight. It sniffs the carcass, then simply plops down on the grass, licking the fur on its back and flicking its tail, like a cat. We hardly move; in fact, we hardly breathe!

After about ten more minutes, a crab-eating fox slips out of the bush to the jaguar's right and pads down to a stream for a drink, or perhaps a meal, clearly upwind of the jag and oblivious of it. The jag quickly senses the fox, arises, and slinks down to where the pond narrows into the stream, keeping a small hill between it and the not-very-sly fox.

The jaguar pauses, crouches, and creeps up the hill. Silently, it launches itself at the fox, landing about a metre short. With amazing reflexes, the fox takes off as the jag is in mid-air, leaps over the stream, and runs directly at us, the jag, as they say, in hot pursuit—about two metres behind.

The fox runs right by us, between the two safari vehicles, and disappears into the darkness behind. The jag stops its chase right in front of us, maybe eight or ten metres away, and stands erect. It stares at us for a long second or two, perhaps deciding whether we are a preferable catch and, easily deconstructed with its powerful jaws, a tastier meal. My first thought: Kefany's easy prey, sitting exposed on the front bumper. My second thought: Oh, no! What if it's looking at me? I'm wearing my brand new western shirt!

The jag seems to eye us contemptuously for several seconds. Is it hunger, or is it disgust, disdain, or frustration? Is it thinking: You bastards just ruined a perfectly good chase! Or: You guys just took an easy meal right out of my mouth! You might be a satisfying alternative. Then it turns on its heel, and, in no hurry, saunters casually through the middle of the shallow pond. In the spotlights we can see that the pond is full of caimans. Dozens of eerie little eyes are reflected in the lights. It is as if the jaguar is defying them to come after it. Without pausing or looking back, it then casually disappears into the woods.

The whole episode lasts about thirty minutes. It is such a rare and thrilling treat that we can hardly talk. Part of the thrill is not just seeing the jag, but being the object of its gaze, being recognized and considered by it. The experience makes me think that we, or at least I, have shared a previously unthinkable bond with a wild creature, have a special relationship with it, one that very few others will ever experience. We had just escaped the routine of everyday life and somehow entered into a different, enchanted realm. Isn't that the true purpose or effect of all travel? To witness animal majesty, to find myself involved with a wild jaguar in a primal way: that's what I'm grateful for.

The next evening, with the aid of a radio tracker, we see a second jaguar. And the following afternoon, a large male walks lazily past the lodge in full daylight. It is close enough that we can see a dab of blood on its flank. It pauses at a tree on the edge of the grassland, turns, and spray it with its scent. Perhaps it lost a territorial fight and was leaving an insolent mark of its reluctant departure.

By the time we leave the Pantanal, we've had close encounters with three tapirs, the ocelot, a jaguarundi, a couple of armadillos, an agouti, some coati mundis, four kinds of deer, some howler monkeys, hundreds of caimans and capybaras and peccaries, and, most importantly of all, three jaguars. Our guides tell us we are the luckiest guests to ever visit the lodge.

Postscript: As dangerous as the encounter with the jaguar might have been, it was nothing compared to the ride we got from the host, Lila Ferrez, at our second lodge in Guapi Assu. When we finished staying at her lodge, she drove us to our final destination. It was a truly harrowing ride.

Lila is an eighty-ish birding enthusiast who drives a small Mitsubishi SUV without functioning seat belts. Three abreast in the back meant one of us had to sit forward on the seat as the car wasn't wide enough for us to sit shoulder to shoulder. Lila, like many Brazilian drivers, believes that road signs and road lines are merely suggestions. She drove like Emerson Fittipaldi, the intrepid Formula One race car driver, i.e. well above the speed limit and often bumper to bumper. She passed sensible drivers on double yellow lines and around blind curves as we held on, white-knuckled, for dear life. She even sped up to pass a motorcycle on a speed bump! We all conked our heads solidly on the ceiling of her car. "It was too dangerous staying behind him," she said, nonchalantly. Unforgettable!

Terrible Trees and Few Birds
A Christmas Story

"CUT YOUR OWN TREE. TWENTY-FIVE CENTS"
The newspaper ad sounded like a challenge to return to the simpler, heartier days of yore. The days before the sixty-five dollar Christmas trees that drop their needles so quickly they look like they've been firebombed three days after you put them up. The days before artificial trees that smell like your basement no matter how much aerosol pine scent you douse them with.

"CUT YOUR OWN TREE." Dream visions of Currier and Ives danced in my head.

I cracked the whip lightly over the head of a gaily blanketed steed. Bells jingled from its harness. Hot breath snorted crystalline from its nostrils. Effortlessly, our sled cut a fresh track through the virgin snow, and frosty billows spangled in our wake. In the back of our sled, next to the gleaming double-bit axe, was a perfectly shaped scotch pine, felled by three vigorous strokes of the axe. Nearby was a pile of freshly cut holly. We sang carols in perfect harmony and joy, and they echoed through the receptive silence as a Great Grey Owl, a cardinal, some Evening Grosbeaks, Whiskey Jacks, and Boreal Chickadees posed obligingly, as if auditioning for spots on our living room tree. Two cute bunny rabbits and a yearling deer, Bambi's identical twin, paused to watch us pass. Coming out of the clearing, we slowed to wave a greeting to … Norman Rockwell, busy at his easel, his pipe a reddening glow against the…

The alarm clock jarred me from this reverie. I groaned a deep, grudging, late-1970s groan. Then I jumped up expectantly. Away to the window I flew like a flash, tripped over the throw rug, and saw through the Venetian blinds that Saturday had dawned grey. Grey as ash. Damp grey. Even Norman Rockwell would have passed it up as unsalvageable.

No problem, I rationalized easily. This is perfect weather for spotting Great Grey Owls. My secret plan was to make this a combination tree-cutting and bird-finding trip. I hadn't been into the boreal forest for quite a while. Maybe I could find a Boreal Chickadee, or an elusive Black-backed Woodpecker, or its cousin the Three-toed. I snuck my binoculars and bird guide into the car.

Instead of a home-made stack of wheat cakes with real maple syrup and tangy country sausage, we decided to make a quick stop for Egg McMuffins so as to get a good head start. But, by the time we were on the Trans-Canada Highway, there was an almost unbroken line of vehicles heading eastward for their own Christmas tree adventure. Our Hornet wagon was between a customized Dodge van and a brand new, black Mercedes casually handled by a guy with Gucci driving gloves. We sang rock'n'roll Christmas songs along with the radio to pump up our slackening enthusiasm.

The Manitoba government-sanctioned tree site was several miles off the TC, along a rutted, narrow, twisting road. By the time we got to the parking lot, the Mercedes had proudly and patiently, car by car, worked itself up to the head of the line. I was almost glad, therefore, to see about 200 cars already in the lot, a bumpy clearing, slick with ice and mud, like chocolate pudding spilled on the floor.

Smoke curled from discarded stumps while trees, rejected at the last minute, were strewn everywhere. Children yelled and/or cried. Dogs howled and tried to yank the bumpers off the cars they were chained to. The persistent, angry growl of overworked gasoline motors—from hundreds of power-saws and snowmobiles—assaulted us. It was like a refugee camp from the Fourth World as painted by Hieronymus Bosch.

Undiscouraged, we chose at random one of the well-trampled trails and set off in search of the perfect tree. The farther into the woods we went, the more we realized this was no simple venture. There were no four-, five-, six-, or even ten-foot trees. Only fifteen-, twenty-, and twenty-five-footers and larger. Axmen had to appraise, chop down, and top these monstrosities to get the living room-sized specimen that one saw being lugged back to the parking lot.

After about a half-mile walk through the woods that reminded me of TV pictures of napalmed targets in Vietnam, we came to a fork in the trail. A Doberman was busy doing what he'd be arrested for doing on the sidewalks of New York. We waited until he bounded off and then watched in stunned silence as three couples dragged their freshly chopped trees right through the spot the dog had just vacated. "Ah, nothing like the fresh smell of the woods on a Christmas morn," they'll no doubt say. "Is the dog around anywhere?"

We knew we were getting close to something when we passed the last of the enterprising boy scouts and hockey players selling hot dogs and cocoa from Coleman stoves and hibachis; the chainsaws and the sporadic oaths of frustrated lumberjacks gave us our second clue.

I left the family on the trail, looped my binocs around my neck, and ventured into an area without any previous footprints. Virgin territory. Not a creature was stirring here. No birds, not even a brave chickadee or a curious crow. No animals. Nothing. The racket had likely scared them all deeper into the woods, perhaps into Ontario.

It was tough going. The snow was waist-deep, the ground uneven, and there were unfrozen puddles of water beneath the snow. Muskeg country. The puddles were about mid-calf-deep and I was wearing hiking shoes that covered my ankles. My wife kept track of where I was by my decreasingly imaginative cursing. A Blue Jay jeered at me. Jay! Jay! Jaȳ! I could have seen him in Winnipeg. The birding part of this adventure was turning sour. Even Roger Tory Peterson himself couldn't have found a bird.

The first tree I chose I dropped in twelve strokes—after inspecting it for nests. No Paul Bunyan feat, but no parlor-game either. The top seven feet or so were green and full—until the tree hit the ground. Then the top three feet broke right off. Too short to use in a house with nine-foot ceilings.

The second tree I felled in about twenty strokes. But its top seven feet had only a single, crooked branch on one side. I rejected it before I topped it. I did the same with the third and fourth trees I dropped. I was pausing between every third or fourth whack by this point. Birding and jogging, I realized, were inadequate training for Christmas tree lumberjacking.

I finally chanced on a twenty-footer that had been cut through almost entirely by a chainsaw but was still standing upright. I felled it with three quick strokes and a mighty shove. It then took me about twenty-five strokes to separate the top seven feet from the rest. In the process, I nearly chopped off a toe and one of the main branches. I also realized that I had slightly miscalculated the fullness and symmetry of this seven-foot top portion. I decided to keep it anyway.

We tried to march triumphantly back to the car, but our hearts just weren't in it. I did start out with a sense of old-fashioned accomplishment. This was no bogus balsam. No fraudulent fir. No paltry parking lot pine. No...

On our way out, the Mercedes driver, seeing my binoculars, asked me whether I'd seen any birds. No, why? Plenty of them back up the trail about fifty metres. Any woodpeckers? Uh, woodpeckers, uh, yeah, plenty. Was he just pulling my chain? My wife gave me a weary nod, and I lit out to find some birds. No luck at all.

We decided to carry the tree out so as not to add to its fragrance and constitution by dragging it along the trail. My wife toted the baby and the top of the tree; I carried the axe and the stump end. We began by exchanging ends, axe, and baby every five minutes or so, resting for a minute while we switched. I used that time to scan the treetops for birds. Again, no luck.

By the time we got back to the car, we were resting for five minutes and changing burdens every minute. We paused to eat charred hot dogs and drink some lukewarm cocoa. A Whiskey Jack eyed me hungrily, interested in my hot dog. At last: a bird! Fresher souls heading past us in search of their own perfect trees seemed to look at us and ours and lose some of their cheeriness and resolve.

On the way back to Winnipeg, I was masochistically calculating how much my twenty-five cent tree had really cost me in gasoline, food, hurt pride, and disillusionment when the black Mercedes Coupe glided past. My eyes glazed over.

The wheels of the Mercedes weren't even touching the highway. The top was down and the driver was beaming. Propped in the backseat between his Abercrombie & Fitch chainsaw and his LL Bean specially designed, Christmas tree chopping outfit was a magnificent, fully proportioned tree. Douglas fir. Suddenly, a quick gust of wind snatched the tree and dashed it under the wheels of an enormous garbage truck. The Mercedes careened out of control and crashed into a passing CN freight train. A Boeing 747 plummeted into the debris. Then Santa Claus and his reindeer flew over with an autopac insurance representative in the back of his sleigh, both of them laughing derisively. Then...

My wife shook me from this delicious daydream just as we drove past our house. I turned around and looked at our meagre coniferous trophy. It seemed fuller and healthier somehow. Its fresh, woodsy smell was more invigorating than before. With some colourful avian ornaments on it, we may have a heart-warming, old-fashioned, birdy Christmas after all.

Things That Don't Make Me Happy, People Who Do

Common Grackles
Unloved and Unwanted

My yard gets overrun by Common Grackles every fall. Scores of them, perhaps eighty or so at a time. It happens at the same time every year. They arrive, scour the lawn for grubs and other grackle delicacies, and move on en masse. I have no idea how they get together, where they come from, or which one decides which yards to invade and when. Maybe my grandson, when he gets to be an enterprising grad student in ornithology, could study this.

Some people consider grackles to be attractive birds. And in a way they are. With their iridescent blue-purple sheen, blazing yellow eyes, and longish, vee-shaped tail, they are distinctive.

But they were *not* attractive to my mother. In fact, she *hated* grackles with a rare fury. The only time I ever heard her curse was when she once snapped, "Those damn grackles!"

Grackles are not musically gifted. The noises they make are among the most grating of any bird. Their raspy squawks sound like iron train wheels on rusty rails. It's hard to call these noises "songs." The birds sound like they're being throttled.

"I do not know which to prefer ... The blackbird whistling/Or just after." That's part of a stanza in Wallace Stevens's great poem "Thirteen Ways of Looking at a Blackbird." He can't be talking about the Yellow-headed Blackbird, the one bird with a "song" worse than a Common Grackle. Unlike Stevens, I know for sure that I do not prefer a grackle's whistling, if that's what people call its "song." I can't wait until the song is over, when peaceful silence erases the squawks. (Great-tailed Grackles of the American South have a much more musical sound than our Common Grackles; a British friend of mine calls them "bubble and squeak" birds. I much prefer their song.)

The sound of just one Common Grackle can be annoying. Many grackles can make a deeply religious woman curse. And you rarely encounter just one grackle. That's because grackles are social nesters, and for many years when I was a child, several grackle families took up residence in the mature blue spruce trees in our front yard. They woke us in the morning, squawked all day, and kept us awake at night.

To make matters worse, the grackle babies, like many birds, create mucous packages for their excretions—called fecal sacs. Their neat-freak parents would remove these sacs from the nest, fly to a convenient body of water, and drop them in. Our family wading pool was a favourite drop-off target. You didn't dare go in the pool if there was one single sac in it. Yuck!

Someone, probably our only neighbour whose kid had a BB gun (we didn't), suggested that we shoot them. Someone else, probably facetiously, suggested that we could then bake them in a pie. The grackles were after all "black" birds, though oddly named, and, with four and twenty to a pie, according to the nursery rhyme, we'd have enough to last us the entire winter. My mom nixed that idea; someone could get their eye shot out. Besides, she hated the noise they made, and the rest of the rhyme goes, "When the pie was opened, the birds began to sing." What an insufferable racket that would've been.

My mom put up with all this until late one summer when more than 100 grackles showed up on our lawn.

To her, this invasion was the last straw, like a scene from Hitchcock's weird horror film *The Birds*. She blamed the spruce trees and demanded that my father get rid of them. He grudgingly obliged—happy to eliminate the birds' homes but unhappy at the lumber-jacking it entailed.

My mom wasn't the only person to hate grackles. If you Google "Getting rid of grackles" you'll find over 100,000 results. Turns out we were lucky. In the southern US, thousands of over-wintering grackles can invade your yard, creating a raucous cacophony of unpleasant sounds. Plus noxious excretions. Lots of people hate those damned grackles!

I myself don't really hate them. I just don't like it when they show up around the tenth of September. Like all black birds from myth and folklore, they are bad omens. Their arrival is prelude to their departure. Gorging themselves on travel fuel from my lawn like long distance runners loading up on carbs before a marathon, they prepare for their southward migration. The grackles are a premature reminder that winter is coming. Winnipeg winters are long enough without two months of depressing anticipation.

Yeah, those damned grackles.

Wrynecks and Other Jinx Birds

By the time you read this, I will *not* have seen a Black-throated Blue Warbler in my home province of Manitoba or a Middle-spotted Woodpecker in Europe or a Wallcreeper anywhere. You may read this ten years from now, and it's likely that I still will not have seen these birds. These are my current jinx birds. I've been searching for them for years.

Jinx birds (some people call them nemesis birds) are those annoying species that all your birding friends have seen but you haven't. To be a jinx, a bird must be difficult to find but not extraordinarily rare, elusive but not impossibly so. (If a rare bird shows up and sticks around for a while, it can qualify as a nemesis bird if many others get to see it and you don't.) It's a bird that you should be able to find but just can't—even with research, dogged dedication, professional help, and prayer. The birding gods conspire against you.

Talking to other birders, I've discovered that almost all of them have jinx birds. My friend Andy Courcelles just cannot find a Barn Owl anywhere in North America; it's not for lack of trying. He now believes that the bird does not actually exist. It's a myth created by smug tormentors or an extinct species like the Carolina Parrot or the Dodo.

Another person I know made nine trips all over the west, including to Alaska and British Columbia, to find a White-tailed Ptarmigan. No luck, the last I heard. Bobwhites have unaccountably eluded people. Also Scaled Quails. Long-eared Owls. Northern Mockingbirds. Ask any birder, and there's usually one species that causes him or her to curse the birding gods.

For many, many years—far too many—my jinx bird was the Black-backed Woodpecker. I made at least two dozen bird trips with this woodpecker as my specific target bird. All were in vain. I even enlisted the help of local experts who scouted appropriate areas (burnt over forests) ahead of time and vowed that a sighting was guaranteed. No luck. For me, the bird was "temporarily extirpated."

It got so bad that I became the butt of jokes whenever birders got together. "Seen a Black-backed yet? Ha. Ha." Or: "Uh oh. Walz is here. No Black-backeds today!" And it was true. I saw the more elusive American Three-toed Woodpecker long before I finally found its near look-alike, the Black-backed.

Sometimes I'd even be on an outing where people would get ahead of the pack or fall behind, and they would see the bird. They'd yell out to the rest of us, but by the time we got to the place they saw the bird, it would have skedaddled. Or they'd mention it at the end of the day. "Oh, by the way, did you guys see the Black-backed?" Duh!

The truly annoying thing is that once people hear about your particular jinx bird, they will line up to tell you about their own sightings of the bird. Usually they will mention how easy it was to find one or how often they've seen it.

Or they will offer advice. "Get to the appropriate habitat at the right time of year and look for *other* birds." Or, "Put the bird completely out of your mind, and it will come to you." Right! Thanks.

Another maddening thing about jinx birds is that once you break the jinx, you will often see the bird everywhere you look. For many years, my European jinx bird was the Golden Oriole. Then one fine day I thought I heard one. So I abandoned my group (they all had already seen one) and struggled through thick foliage, thorn bushes, and swampy grounds for thirty minutes. The oriole, hearing my noisy, profane pursuit, kept flitting just enough ahead to elude me.

Finally, battered, bleeding, and wet-soxed, I tracked it down. A wonderful bird—more brilliantly lemon-coloured than golden but a stunner. Well worth the effort.

When I finally made my way back to the group, I discovered that they had just had close-up views of six Golden Orioles from the comfort of a roadside rest area! AARRGH!

It's a cruel joke that above all others, even the pesky Golden Oriole, the European jinx bird that eluded me for the longest time was the oddly named Eurasian Wryneck. I searched for it more than a dozen times. In vain. Then Christian Artuso, the person who captained the Manitoba Breeding Bird Atlas even though he was not originally from this province, heard about my Wryneck frustrations. He told me I should have looked around the Colosseum in Rome; they were plentiful there. I'd visited the Colosseum, even had my binoculars with me. I never thought to check out the birds in the vicinity. I thought they were just House Sparrows!

On my thirteenth (lucky) Wryneck search in northern Germany, I finally eliminated it as a jinx bird. Believe it or not, its Latinate name is *Jynx torquilla*. I kid you not!

What's in a Name?

Several years ago, when I heard that the brainiacs responsible for naming birds were going to split the Winter Wren into two separate species, my biggest fear was that they were going to name one of them the Wilson's Wren. It all goes back to the time they changed the Common Snipe into the Wilson's Snipe. Why not just call it a Snipe, like every gullible Boy Scout who ever hunted one? Or the American Snipe (to distinguish it from the European version). Even the Gutter Snipe would have been preferable!

If ever there was a guy who didn't need another bird named after him, it's this guy Wilson.

Think of it: Wilson's Storm-Petrel, Wilson's Plover, Wilson's Phalarope, Wilson's Snipe, Wilson's Warbler, Wilson's Thrush (now, thankfully, changed to Veery).

Over sixty North American birds are named after people, and ten percent of them are named after Wilson. His two nearest competitors have only three—Cassin (Murrelet, Finch, and Sparrow) and Swainson (Hawk, Thrush, and Warbler). Do the namers have no imagination?

Who is this guy Wilson? He's Alexander Wilson—one of America's great early ornithologists and painters. In his celebrated pre-Audubon work, the nine-volume *American Ornithology* (1808–1814), he illustrated 268 species of birds, twenty-six of which had not previously been described. So, it's good that we honour him. I just hope that we don't end up someday with all twenty-six bearing his name!

Gene Walz

A friend of mine once facetiously suggested that we name birds more accurately or more "phylogenetically-aligned." He proposed the House Weaver (for House Sparrow) and Canada Brant (Canada Goose) for starters; then he got carried away and proposed the White-headed and -tailed Fish-Eagle (replacing the Bald one), the Rusty-bellied Lawn Thrush (the American Robin), and the Orange-crowned Chicken-strutting Ground-warbler (the Ovenbird). Another facetious birder once suggested that the Red-breasted Nuthatch should really be called the "Soft Rusty/Orange Wash-breasted Nuthatch." It's an amusing game. But bird names are odd enough as it is.

If we haven't crossed paths for a while, Syl, a longtime friend of mine, almost always asks me if I've seen any Rosy-breasted Pushovers lately. This is a typical non-birder to birder joke; birds with "funny" names often provoke snickers and smirks. Once, when I told him I'd just seen a Hoary Redpoll, his reply was, "Whoring Red Poles? There are actual birds with that name? That's obscene! Or at least politically incorrect."

When I was a kid without a bird book, I had my own personal names for the birds I saw. For instance, I called Common Yellowthroats Masked Bandits. And my grandson Torsten, you'll remember, called Nuthatches Upside-down Birds. Maybe we should let preschoolers re-name birds. It might get them interested in the outdoors.

More seriously, we should change the names of birds that are just not descriptively accurate. The Red-bellied Woodpecker, for instance. Its belly is the least distinctive characteristic of the bird and often what little red there is isn't visible at all. Or the Ring-necked Duck which should be the Ring-billed Duck. I'm even tempted to petition for the Orange-crowned Warbler (whose crown you almost never see) to be re-named the Dull Green Warbler. There are dozens more.

When I get to be president of the American Ornithologists' Union (just after I become the first agnostic Pope!), I'm going to institute a checklist committee with a mandate to start re-naming birds. First rule: no more than one species can have a person's name attached to it. Maybe even drop all surnames attached to birds. Think of all the publicity it'll generate and all the fun we'll have cooking up more imaginative, helpful, and apt names!

When it comes to naming animals, the Aussies have been the most creative. We could take our cue from them. Just saying the names they've come up with can make you smile. What we call a kingfisher, for instance, they call a kookaburra. And then there are their animals: platypus, pademelon, bandicoot, wombat, wallaby, echidna. What great names! Even their really familiar animals have memorably amusing names: kangaroo, koala, dingo, and Tasmanian devil. Some unfamiliar ones are even funnier: numbat, quoll, bilby, quokka.

I wish we could get a do-over not just on bird names but on all our North American animal names. They're all so monosyllabic and uninspiring. Bear, deer, fox, wolf, moose, elk, hare. Was there some kind of prohibition in the past that limited the number of syllables you could use to name our fauna?! Government accountants must have named them.

As for the changeover to Canada Brant from Canada Goose: I think I'd prefer that we change the name to New Jersey Brant or Lawn-fouling Brant. The pesky birds have become such a menace in parks and golf courses in the last several years that we Canadians should officially disown them. Like the "cold fronts from Canada" that TV weather forecasters all decry, the Canada Goose is giving us a bad name.

The Passenger Pigeon
Apocalypse

Every fall, the Committee on the Status of Endangered Wildlife in Canada (COSEWIC) meets to assess the risk of extinction for Canadian wildlife species. At these meetings, the Birds Specialist Subcommittee presents status reports for threatened or endangered bird species. It must be depressing work. We hear all the time about the growing percentages of at-risk birds. A massive seven-year climate study, for instance, finds that unless action is taken, more than 300 species of North American birds could face significant threats to their survival in coming decades. (The international figures are worse: over 3,000 species, almost one-third, of all bird species, could be extinct by 2050.)

Greater Prairie-Chicken, a bird that once numbered in the millions on the grasslands: extirpated in Canada; Eskimo Curlew and Mountain Plover: endangered; Burrowing Owl, as late as the 1980s a resident just outside Winnipeg: virtually extirpated in Manitoba; Yellow Rail and Savannah Sparrow (the *princeps* or "Ipswich" subspecies): of special concern. Also in trouble: Sprague's Pipit, Dickcissel, and Loggerhead Shrike, to cite just three species of special interest to Manitobans.

Over the past fifty years, grassland birds especially have suffered alarming reductions, some by more than ninety percent. As a group, they are declining faster than any other species on the continent. Humans, the most dangerous of the invasive species on the prairies, are entirely responsible.

More brutally and foolishly, humans were also responsible for the demise of the Passenger Pigeon. If you look at the award-winning *Birds of Manitoba*, you'll see that the Passenger Pigeon has an entry in the book. It was once a frequent and abundant visitor to our province. Its entry in the Birds of Manitoba is unique. It's an obituary, a lament, and, perhaps, a warning, the only one in the book.

The story of this species' extinction, including its former occurrence in Manitoba, has been told many times. But it bears repeating—especially now, just after the 100th anniversary of its demise. In "A Review-History of the Passenger Pigeon in Manitoba" written in 1905, Winnipeg ornithologist George Atkinson called North American civilization a form of "modified barbarism" for its wanton extermination of the species, an act of human greed and selfishness. Over a century later, we don't seem to have progressed beyond his apt description: "modified barbarism." It is still difficult to read or write about the Passenger Pigeon without stirring strong emotions.

Emotions such as incredulity, because the Passenger Pigeon once numbered in the billions—as many as three to five billion—with a "b"— representing a quarter of all the birds on the North American continent. It was likely the most numerous bird species on the entire planet. As late as 1871, a colony of 136 million birds was discovered nesting in central Wisconsin. Migrating flocks were said to darken the sky, horizon to horizon, for entire days.

And emotions like disappointment, because the Passenger Pigeon was a truly beautiful bird whose speed and grace in flight earned it such names as "blue meteor." Chief Simon Pokagon—poet, naturalist, and early critic of pigeon hunting—claimed that it "was proverbial with our fathers that if the Great Spirit in His wisdom could have created a more elegant bird in plumage, form, and movement, He never did."

At forty centimetres in length, the Passenger Pigeon was markedly larger than the Mourning Dove, with a similar build, including a long, pointed tail. The male, more richly coloured than the female, had a slaty, blue-grey head and upper body with purplish iridescence on the neck; its throat and breast were, as Atkinson put it, a "rich russet vinaceous" colour that shaded to orange-pink on the lower breast and then a white abdomen. It was also unique of voice, reportedly the only pigeon that "shriek[ed] and chatter[ed] and cluck[ed] instead of cooing."

Their extinction should make us all angry because it was unfettered human greed that obliterated this ill-fated species, its breeding cycle totally disrupted by widespread annual slaughters. Hundreds of tons of pigeon carcasses were shipped by rail to city restaurants and markets. Tragically, many were simply discarded. This continued unabated up to and beyond the last great nesting in Michigan in 1878, even as belated warnings of extinction were being sounded.

And it should make us feel terribly sad because this prodigiously gregarious species, whose nesting colonies once extended up to 1000 or more square kilometres, was finally extinguished with the lonely, pathetic death of a single bird called Martha, the last known Passenger Pigeon, in the Cincinnati Zoological Gardens on September 1, 1914. Although the species bred readily in captivity, the last captive birds were descendants of a single pair captured in 1888, so inbreeding precluded any eleventh-hour miracle.

Records compiled by several authorities indicate that the Passenger Pigeon was a more abundant migrant in the settled portions of Manitoba. A tolerably common summer resident of the wooded regions of the province, its range extended north of lakes Manitoba and Winnipeg, with sporadic sightings around Hudson Bay at York Factory and possibly Churchill. Its presence was noteworthy enough that there is a Pigeon Rapids, Manitoba named after the bird.

The birds arrived in the province as early as mid-April, but mainly in May, and remained until October. Voracious eaters of deciduous forest mast in eastern North America, their nomadic movements and concentrated breeding revolved around the sporadic abundance of beechnut, acorns, and chestnuts. They fed extensively on acorns and wild berries in Manitoba, but also became significant agricultural pests.

Nesting colonies in Manitoba were not as wildly extensive as they were in Pennsylvania, Michigan, and Wisconsin where nest sites were legendary for their size and density. Colonies could be scores of miles long with some trees sagging and branches breaking under the weight of the birds and their flimsy nests. Passenger Pigeons were sufficiently abundant near the south end of Lake Winnipeg, however, to furnish a subsistence diet for Aboriginal people in summer, between the spring sturgeon runs and the fall wild-rice harvest. Nesting localities mentioned by famed naturalist and writer Ernest Thompson Seton included the Red River Valley, Ossowa (near Poplar Point), Portage la Prairie, along the Waterhen and Shell Rivers, and probably Carberry. Eggs were also collected at Oak Lake and the southwest shore of Lake Manitoba.

Passenger Pigeons were first reported in Manitoba in 1827 by Arctic explorer and naturalist Sir John Richardson, and they were evidently abundant in Manitoba in the 1850s. But a marked decline was noticeable by 1870, and the species last came to the province in some force in 1878. The species had all but disappeared by 1885, although hundreds of dozens were reportedly still going to market from "Indian Territory" in Manitoba as late as 1892. Norman Criddle reported a forlorn male near Treesbank on September 21, 1902, one of a handful of plausible early 20th century reports. After this, nothing.

To see Passenger Pigeons now, you have to go to the Manitoba Museum; four specimens are preserved there. Two eggs and two skins from Manitoba are also housed at the University of California, Berkeley, one egg and one skin from this province are at the Royal Ontario Museum in Toronto, and one egg is at the Smithsonian Museum in Washington, DC. They could be the centre of an exhibit in the Canadian Museum for Human Rights in Winnipeg.

From billions and billions of birds to a few preserved skins and eggs; and it took less than half a century. What a record!

If there is a lesson to be learned, it is not the simple one that we must not take natural abundance for granted. Passenger Pigeons were exterminated because they were easily slaughtered and were a profitable commodity. In an era when many species are endangered and the environment is under attack, we must make it difficult and expensive for profiteers to squander and deplete our natural resources.

Bird Feeder Freeloaders

Despite the title of this section, I am not a grumpy guy, just occasionally testy, petulant, "out of sorts." There are too many grumpy guys in the world. Just look at TV cop shows: *Criminal Minds*, *Law & Order*, and *CSI* all feature old guys with bad dispositions. Whenever I feel a bout of negativity or crabbiness coming on, I turn on one of those shows and tell myself to chill.

But one thing really gets my dander up: squirrels! If you've got a bird feeder or two, your biggest enemy is the squirrel. Squirrel-proof bird feeders! Ha! Nothing works. No self-respecting bird book would be complete without some mention of squirrels.

I've (mostly) learned to live with the pesky rodents. I'm not a crotchety, old coot who sits on his deck with a BB gun or a water rifle full of ammonia. I don't begrudge them the sunflower seeds and peanuts they work so cleverly to extract from my supposedly squirrel-proof feeders. What annoys me is when the squirrels dominate the feeders. The birds have to wait their turn, and during the wait, the birds are vulnerable to other predators—hawks, shrikes, and free-range cats. Squirrels are also more direct enemies of birds; they steal eggs from nests and even kill young birds. Although I figure it's a trade-off, since hawks take down squirrels, too.

So, when I came acros a blog titled "100 Dead Squirrels," I laughed with glee. "Great," I thought, "100 fewer squirrels left in the world. It's a start." Sad to say, the title of the blog was misleading.

To me, red and grey and black squirrels are not, as my daughters claim, cute. Let's be frank here: they're just rats with flexible, fluffy tails. Rats who prefer trees to sewers and have no fear of heights. Rats who could probably work for Cirque du Soleil if they could fit into tiny, colourful spandex outfits. Destructive tree rats.

One night, when my daughters were teenagers, they complained to me that the upstairs bathroom fan was not working. Bathrooms are sacred areas to teenagers. I had to act quickly. So I grabbed a stepladder, put on my handyman face and gloves, and removed the fan. As I did, two gallons of acorns cascaded down on me. Plus other assorted bits of debris and dozens of maggots, the larder of a red squirrel. The little red monster had chewed through the vent cap and set up his winter home in the pipe.

Two weeks later, my clothes dryer croaked. Evicted from the bathroom vent pipe, the red devil had built a new nest in the dryer vent, preventing the heat from escaping and cooking the dryer. That cost me big bucks.

I set up a live trap to catch it, but caught a grey squirrel instead. Fine. It was the guy who had gnawed his way through three two-by-fours on my deck. I drove him ten miles away and dumped him in a park. To make a long story short, I caught ten more grey squirrels before I called in an exterminator. He caught three more before he got a little red one. One grey had gnawed his way into the attic, one had chewed a hole into the soffits. More $$ gone!

Then another red squirrel chewed through the roof of my tool shed. Rain and snow came in before I discovered the hole. I was momentarily amazed at the fancy digs he'd set up: a place for his acorns, a separate place for his crab apples, another spot for his pine cones, another for his bedroom, and another for his latrine. His carpentry rotted the floor, wrecked the place. More $$$ gone.

But he had a weakness for peanut butter, and we caught him.

As the exterminator carted off the red monster, his parting advice was: "You've got a yard full of oak trees. It's a squirrel magnet. Find a couple of squirrels you like and learn to live with them." He sold me his live trap.

I'm still trying to find a squirrel I like.

Bird-Guiding
Not as Tempting as It Seems

Whenever Winnipeg winters got too much for me or my job got me down, I would fantasize about ditching everything to become a bird guide in some warm, sunny place. Costa Rica, for instance, or Ecuador, Brazil, Thailand, or Australia. Warm climates, lots of birds. Ah!

For an avid birder, could there possibly be a better job?

Bird-guiding can be delightful—sharing your knowledge of birds and helping novices identify beautiful winged creatures and discover the joys of birding while enjoying the great outdoors. I love going into the woods with my grandson and teaching him about birds, pointing out where they can be found, what strange habits they have, and how they're different from one another. He's a keen, inquisitive student with active eyes, sensitive ears, and lots of patience.

But being a professional bird guide isn't all it's cracked up to be.

To be an expert bird guide, you have to be able to quickly identify each bird you see or hear. You have to point out the precise characteristics that led to the identification—sometimes an almost impossible task as the distinctions can be miniscule. (In Craig Robson's *The Birds of Southeast Asia*, for instance, there is an entire page of warblers that, to the inexperienced eye, look exactly the same.) And you have to point out the exact location of the bird so that everyone can find it before it flits away and often train a spotting scope on the bird for all to see it in close-up. Not at all easy!

But the birds are not always the problem. It's the wannabe bird observers that can drive a guide nuts. Some people can't even see birds lined up full-frame in a spotting scope; some can't hear birds two feet away from them.

After doing some bird-guiding around Manitoba, I soon realized that it would be easier for me to become quarterback for the Winnipeg Blue Bombers (sometimes I think I should audition!) than for some people to become proficient birders.

Some people just aren't meant to be birders. People, for instance, that I like to call the Whazzats. These are earnest people who can hear sounds but can't locate or identify them. Sometimes it's the sound of a truck backing up, or a common bird like a robin way off in the distance. There's usually one on each bird outing. Every time they hear even the slightest sound, they immediately ask, "Whazzat?!" In fact, it's usually not a question but a command. This can drive even the most patient bird guide batty.

I once asked another, more expert guide what his least favourite guiding experiences were. He told me about the Shoveler Lady. He was guiding a group at Oak Hammock Marsh and was starting with the ducks there, very easy to identify. Of all the ducks, the Northern Shovelers are perhaps the easiest of all to identify. Their distinctive green, brown, and white markings and oversized bills are hard to miss, and their names are hard to forget as well. (Northern Pintails are pretty recognizable too. They have distinctive pin-tails.) But one novice birder kept pointing out different shovelers and asking the guide what they were. "What's that funny-looking bird there, the one with the oversized bill?" After the third time, he thought she was pulling his leg. But she wasn't. He resisted the urge to say, "It's another shoveler, you twit!" That would have been bad bird-guiding protocol. Instead, he patiently pointed her in the direction of other birds that were more interesting to look at.

If you've ever been in a van with other birders on an outing, you've probably gritted your teeth at birders who work on a different concept of time than everyone else. They lag behind the group and are sometimes five or even fifteen minutes late returning to a van. Everyone else must wait for them. Or they insist on sitting next to the side door of a van and blocking everyone else from getting out while they check something in their bag. They drive bird guides nuts!

On a recent bird trip to Vietnam, a photographer with a huge camera lens would subtly bump people out of the way to get a better picture of a bird. I got elbowed twice as I caught my first glimpses of "life-birds," ones I'd never seen before and likely would never see again. I wanted to throttle the guy or at least drop his camera into a ravine. We had words. By the end of the trip, we all wanted to throttle him!

Then there's the person who won't shut up. Or can't speak at less than volume ten on his or her dial. He or she sees the bird outing as a social occasion, a place to catch up on the latest gossip or even talk politics. European Union? Not even slightly interested, I'm afraid! The Kardashians? Lord, save me!

Or the constant complainer. He/she uses every slight or unusual challenge as an opportunity to moan and groan. "This path is too rocky! Can't we take another break? We've been going too fast!" Or uses the final evaluation as a chance to vent about the most trivial problems. Lord help the guide that doesn't find the bird that a complainer "needs!" I've been party to both. It ain't pretty.

Then there's the constant caviler who feels the need to dispute your identifications with no evidence and little experience. "Are you absolutely sure that isn't a Magnolia Warbler?" Or "That looks more like a Wood Thrush to me!" And usually in a querulous tone of voice.

I've even been on trips with people who can't help bragging—at the most inappropriate times—about all the birds they've seen and all the places they've been. "Oh, that reminds me of the ibis I saw on the Brahmaputra River back in 1999. It's the most glorious bird, much better than other…" and on and on and on.

I used to consider myself a pretty expert identifier of birds and birdsong. I thought that I could retire and maybe devote some of my days to bird-guiding in the tropics. I now realize that expertise isn't enough. A bird guide has to be a teacher, a psychologist, a nurse, a cop, a diplomat, a counselor, a navigator, an intercessor, a food consultant if in a foreign land, and many other things as the occasions arise.

Maybe I'm not cut out to be a bird guide unless it's with a few carefully chosen, compatible people, in some hyper-birdy locale on a perfect, hot, sunny day. Maybe I should just content myself with being a mentor to my two grandsons. They don't complain. They don't argue. And they've got quicker eyes than me. That's good enough for me.

Nerdy?
No Way!

Nerdy. That's how a reporter characterized the group of people who assembled in River Heights in the summer of 2014 to catch sight of a pair of Mississippi Kites that seemed to magically show up there, thousands of kilometres from their ordinary range.

Nerdy! I don't know about you, but this, to me, is not a compliment. Nerds, aka geeks, are people who are socially clumsy, physically weak, psychologically inadequate, or narrowly focussed. Foolish caricatures. The birders I know are anything but.

I wonder if this careless reporter was even on the scene to see the birders he so casually dissed. What I saw when I was there (and I showed up often and never saw a reporter) were lawyers, some doctors and nurses, an engineer, a landscaper, a luthier, a former TV technician, a farmer, a handyman, some school teachers and profs, government workers, secretaries, several retirees from all walks of life, and other ordinary folks. I doubt any one of them would self-identify as a nerd, if pressed. Well, maybe facetiously as a "bird nerd" because of the amusing assonance. However, I personally took offense at the nerd word. Clearly this guy was falling back on old, discredited stereotyping rather than even perfunctory observation or elementary-school research.

Google, for instance, indicates that US president Teddy Roosevelt, the original tough-guy Rough Rider, was a birder. He once criticized famous naturalist John Muir for not knowing birdsongs as well as he did. Call him a nerd?

Or how about Wes Craven, the maestro of horror movies. The writer/director of *Scream* and *A Nightmare on Elm Street* and all their scary sequels was a birder.

Fidel Castro is a birder. So is Prince Philip. And US president Jimmy Carter.

Michael J. Fox, Daryl Hannah, Steve Martin, and Cameron Diaz are birders. And, it is said, Mick Jagger and Paul McCartney. So too are novelists Ian Fleming, Jonathan Franzen, Margaret Atwood, Timothy Findley, and David Arnason as well as writer George Plimpton who once suited up as a goalie for the Boston Bruins, played quarterback for the Detroit Lions, and got knocked silly by boxing champ Sugar Ray Robinson. All are birders and not a nerd in the bunch.

When I returned to serious birding as a grad student, one of the things that kept me interested was the fact that the birders I met were from all walks of life, including a cop, a gas station owner, and an ex-football player. They came in all shapes, sizes, races, and genders. It was an invigorating cross-section of people. There were some weirdos, I guess, as there are in every hobby and social group. But these birders were real people with interesting lives, outdoorsy and outgoing.

Birding is not an extreme sport, but there are risks that every birder understands more than most people. Ticks and mosquitoes with their communicable diseases, Lime disease and West Nile, and plants with their poison ivy and nettles. Farther abroad: snake bites and animal attacks, hepatitis, malaria, zika virus and dengue fever. It's not a hobby for the timid.

Helping my grandsons find and identify birds, their behaviours, and the environments they frequent, however, is not dangerous. It's a fun thing to do. But I'm not trying to make them into birders, just observers of nature who are comfortable outdoors and alert to its power, variety, and beauty. Birds are messengers from another realm. Through them, I hope people learn to love and respect nature and the outdoors—experience some of the delight, wonder, and awe that I have. If my grandsons do become lifelong birders, that's a bonus. It sure beats sitting in a dark basement experiencing nature second-hand—on a screen. It pains me to hear that the only tweets that kids experience these days are on their Twitter accounts on their computers.

If my grandsons do become birders, I hope they are not stigmatized by ignorant bullies who mistakenly categorize them as nerds. There are trolls and shamers out there who will do anything to slake the thirst of their stunted egos. They think that watching endless sports on TV makes them somehow more manly or normal. It's bad enough that stifled people sit around and use their computers to bash and critique people they don't know. To find a reporter slinging casual insults is reprehensible. Oh, oh. I'm starting to sound like a grumpy old man. I'd better say something nice about him. Hmmm. Well, at least his grammar is flawless.

The Old Man and the Lek

Birding is not just about finding birds and ticking them off your life list. It's about the spiritually replenishing experience of being outdoors, seeing other kinds of fauna and flora, and meeting other wacky and wonderful people.

To get that full-value birding experience, you have to go to Colorado to see the prairie chickens. These birds are among the great, eccentric performers in the world, and besides, the scenery there is magnificent, the animals (pronghorns, elk, moose, bighorn sheep, etc.) are not terribly difficult to find, and you'll meet some memorable folks while you're at it.

Fred Dorenkamp is one of those memorable characters. Fred was a professional rodeo cowboy for forty years, specializing in bronc busting. He also ran a Colorado rodeo company and was a livestock contractor with bucking broncs and mean bulls that left their marks on many cowboy riders. Tall, raw-boned, and toughened from dust-bowl summers and fearsome winters, Fred hardly shows his 80-plus years. A lifelong rancher, he now owns and operates a local convenience store, is a self-described "chief bottle-washer" at the county fair, and runs Arena Dust Tours, where he serves, in his words, as a "chicken-rider."

Fred doesn't ride barnyard chickens—he rides people to wild ones. In his well-worn-in Stetson, blue jeans, and flannel shirt, he leads birding tours to find endangered prairie chickens.

He's been monitoring Lesser Prairie Chickens in the vicinity of his

Lamar, Colorado ranch for many years. They're endangered grassland birds and if they survive, it'll be because of Fred and people like him.

Lesser Prairie Chickens have been dancing on ancestral leks for eons. These leks are the bird-equivalent of '70s singles bars. They're places where horny, amped-up young males assemble to impress the few hot young females that show up. They usually outnumber the females about five or six to one. Sometimes more.

To see these prairie chickens you have to arrive at their secret, remote leks well before dawn in March and April. That means getting up at 4:00 am and meeting Fred for a ride through pitch darkness to a grassy field in the middle of nowhere. You ride in a bouncy school bus that's only somewhat younger than Fred. It's uncomfortable and full of people, parkas, backpacks, and spotting scopes.

Before you get to the lek, Fred presents his rules. In a growly, nasal voice worthy of a cartoon character, he tells you: keep quiet and keep still. Any noise or movement will spook the birds. The only sounds as you approach the lek are your bones rattling as the spring-less bus heads across the bumpy terrain.

After an hour of anxious waiting, the lek is bright enough that a few dark shadows appear. The performances are already underway.

The males strut around, they stomp, they scurry, they bow and shuffle, they jump up and down, and they fight. They puff out their gaudily-coloured throat patches, they erect their head feathers so they look like horns, and they rattle their wings. If you can get close enough, you can hear them cackle and coo.

While you are all mesmerized and amused by these weird dances, the female prairie chickens hardly seem impressed. But eventually, after a couple of weeks of watching, they'll find suitable mates.

After an hour or so, the birds all fly off, and you head back to Fred's ranch. His cattle dog Bella greets you, and you are ushered into a low shed where his wife Norma has prepared a full ranch breakfast. Bacon, sausages, eggs, toast, dumplings and gravy, juice and coffee. (No beans.) Your group almost feels like cowboys and cowgirls.

The breakfast room features a stuffed prairie chicken and a large colour photograph for those days when the real live birds don't show up. But you can't add a taxidermist's work to your life list. Nor is the experience quite the same.

Later on during the day that I was there, Fred hitched his horses up to a buckboard and transported a coffin from a nearby church to the local cemetery. He'll probably go out the same way. But I hope he has many good years before then—to help protect the prairie chickens and to shepherd birders to the leks.

Old Jack
and the Crow with One Leg

I first met Jack Foster in April 1997 when he phoned me to help identify a bird that he'd spotted at his feeders. I lived down the street, two blocks away. He had videotaped a large dove and wasn't quite sure what it was; he just knew it was different. And if his guess was right, it shouldn't be in Manitoba. That's what made him call me.

The bird was a Band-tailed Pigeon, only the fifth ever seen in Manitoba. Jack was naturally thrilled to be the first to find this rare bird. It was only then that I discovered his backyard full of feeders. He admitted he wasn't an expert on birds, but he was enthusiastic enough that I recruited him as a feeder observer for the annual Christmas Bird Count. Thus began a fruitful birding friendship.

Jack was a small man, maybe five-foot-two, with oversized glasses from the 1970s, a thin comb-over that didn't fool anyone, and a fashion sense that favoured mismatched plaids. However, Jack was living proof that looks can be deceiving. He was the kind of guy my uncle Pete would have affectionately called a "tough old nutter"—wiry, curious, undaunted.

His career as an engineer took him to many of the danger zones of Africa and the Middle East. His sense of adventure led him to hand-build and then pilot his own version of a Cessna airplane. When he retired he researched and built precise replicas of various ships he'd read about; he somehow found the original construction plans and scaled them down. No kits for him!

Jack lived next to a couple that had let their yard run wild. All their weeds and bushes attracted birds; so Jack decided to feed them. Over the years, his feeders attracted more than his fair share of rarities. Whenever he came across a bird he wasn't sure of, he'd videotape it and phone me. I could never get out of his house very quickly. His tapes were too long and his stories too fascinating.

Jack had feeders of all descriptions—sunflower seeds, peanut butter, millet, niger seeds, sugar water, oranges, bread, you name it. He fed everything from hummingbirds to starlings, orioles to sparrows. But his favourite stash of food he reserved for a crow with only one leg.

That crow returned at about the same time every year, like the swallows to Capistrano and the turkey vultures to Hinckley, Ohio. As soon as the bird got back, he'd sit on Jack's picnic table cawing for food. Jack fed him left over table scraps and dog food. As a special treat, he'd cook up a hot dog, chop it into bite-sized bits, and arrange them in a row on his picnic table. If ever there was a symbiotic relationship, this was it.

When Jack died, his wife moved into a care home. Their children got rid of the bird feeders at a garage sale and sold the house. The new owners still don't have any feeders at all, and they're probably still annoyed at the insistent cawing of a one-legged crow in their backyard. I saw him in the spring following Jack's death. Somehow, he'd outlived his hardy old pal Jack.

All over the world people fill and re-fill bird feeders, and they take special delight in noting the birds that frequent them. Some feeder-stockers can even identify specific birds that come at regular, predictable times of day. They even give those birds individual names. (Jack didn't.) My mother, for instance, fed pieces of bread to a Ring-necked Pheasant that came twice a day our side door. She named it Gus. Why did she do it? Why do people feed birds?

Birds do take some nourishment from feeders, especially during cold, snowy stretches when their natural foods disappear. But feeders are more for the benefit of the people who stock them than for the birds that use them. Bird feeders provide a way for people to connect to the outside world, to the natural world. Jack knew that, even though he anthropomorphized that one-legged crow and treated him more like a friend than a wild creature. Birds at your feeders can certainly brighten your darkest day.

Bob Taylor
The Funniest Birder Ever

The Carnivore Restaurant in Nairobi, Kenya is a meat-lover's paradise. It serves all the usual domestic meats, and, when available, the more exotic game animals, legally obtained "bush meat": crocodile, camel, wildebeest, ostrich, zebra, guinea fowl, and maybe warthog. We had tasted ostrich (like tough chicken), crocodile (like tougher chicken), and camel (like I don't know what, maybe leather sandals), when a waiter approached in his black-and-white, zebra-skinned apron. He asked if we'd like to try some zebra. "Yes," said Bob Taylor, quick as a flash, "but just the dark meat." We all groaned.

Several days earlier, he had told us about the time when he and a couple of friends had gotten up early to try to spot some leopards. "But when we found them, they were already spotted," he said with a straight face. Groan.

Robert Taylor—Bwana Bob when he led African safaris—did not care if his jokes and puns made us groan as much as laugh. He was a fearless and naturally funny guy.

Michael J. Fox is a funny actor and a birder. But he is not a funny birder. Comedian Steve Martin is a birder and plays a birder in the amusing movie *The Big Year*; he's a funny man. But he is not a funny birder. Bob Taylor was a funny birder.

On a bird walk with Bob one rainy summer day, we came upon a very bedraggled Blue Jay. Not only was it soaking wet, it was also missing a bunch of feathers, including most of its distinctive crest. "Sad-looking jay," I remarked. "Looks crestfallen to me," was Bob's immediate retort. In Africa, when we spotted a Secretary Bird—like a cross between an egret and an eagle (a large grey bird, five feet tall, with long legs, black above the knee, a long tail, the head of a raptor with an orange facial mask and black plumes like a feathery mullet)—Bob quipped "That bird is too absurd for words"—with emphasis on the rhyme.

Not all of his humor was so "refined." Once while driving to check out winter birds east of Winnipeg, we heard an ad for Viagra on the car radio. It warned about calling your doctor if you had an erection lasting for more than four hours. Bob announced, "I know a lot more people I'd phone before I called my doctor."

Bob was quick-witted but he also had some well-honed jokes that he was unafraid to insert into a conversation if given the opportunity. Sitting at a dinner table with a beer in front of him, he'd say, "I'd rather have a bottle in front of me than a frontal lobotomy." On another occasion, he said that he once had a trained cat that would eat cheese and sit next to a mouse hole "with baited breath." After an unsuccessful search for lions that could climb trees in Tanzania, he told us we'd been on the first truthful day of the trip: "No lyin!'"

The safaris he led to Tanzania and Kenya were extraordinarily well-planned, the game drives producing close-ups with all of the "charismatic megafauna" (elephants, rhinos, hippos, lions, leopards, etc.) and exotic native birds, but also wonderful tent camps and lodges for his groups to settle into. But he also knew how to handle people and emergencies. When one of our group contracted food poisoning, Bob arranged to have him flown to a hospital in Nairobi in less than an hour. (The guy recovered.) And when a lodge summarily cancelled all of our reservations in favour of a higher-paying group, he found a much better lodge nearby.

At lunch or dinner at these camps, when talk turned invariably to flying, he'd confess, "I'm a nervous flyer. You arrive at a 'terminal,' and you're constantly reminded of 'departures.'" When one couple announced that they were stopping in Egypt on the way back from his Kenyan safari, Bob asked whether they were going on one of those tours where everyone is forced to eat beans all day. "So they can toot in common."

Bob also led birding and polar bear tours to Churchill, Manitoba. In fact, he was one of the first to do so. My wife and I went there one

Halloween, unaware that Bob was there leading a tundra buggy tour. When we got back, he didn't castigate us for choosing the tour's assigned guide instead of him, he simply asked us whether we'd seen any "pa-tar-migans in the pa-tamaracks." I had to force my eyes from rolling.

Bob was so genial and comfortable around people, you could forget that he'd spent hours and hours alone studying and photographing birds and animals. He was not reluctant to share his knowledge about birds or anecdotes about his experiences. He once told me about watching wood-peckers in the rain and discovering that they could lock their talons into a tree trunk right under a thick branch and fall asleep for the night protected and perfectly dry.

Bob had the perfect temperament to be a birder and naturalist. He was carefully observant, imaginative, empathetic, and, above all, patient. These are the qualities that made him such a wonderful photographer, wood carver, and birding companion. He didn't just observe birds to build a list of life-sightings or firsts. He watched them carefully and at length until he understood them. In a way, he seemed to relate to them—especially the solitariness of his two iconic figures: the Great Grey Owl and the Polar Bear.

He translated this understanding of wildlife into stunning photographs for numerous national and international magazines, including such familiar ones as *LIFE*, *Canadian Geographic*, *Reader's Digest*, *Equinox*, *International Wildlife*, and *Outdoor Photography Canada*, among others. His books have central positions on many bookshelves and coffee tables. *The Edge of the Arctic: Churchill and the Hudson Bay Lowlands*; *The Manitoba Landscape: A Visual Symphony*; *The Great Gray Owl on Silent Wings*; and *Manitoba: Seasons of Beauty*. His photography earned him an impressive list of accolades. He is one of the few photographers, for instance, to be accepted into the Royal Canadian Academy of Arts. But he was a kind of Renaissance Man: photographer, sculptor, filmmaker, painter, lecturer, curator, raconteur, and good friend to many.

After a long hike with Bob one day, watching birds and sharing stories, I complained that my knees were killing me. Bob said he had the same problem and that doctors had diagnosed it as knee-monia. On another outing he complained about his weight. "Look at this belly," he complained. "I must be anorexic." Gullible me: "Anorexic!? Why?" Bob:

"Because the definition of an anorexic is a person who looks in a mirror and thinks they're fat."

Ironically it was his belly that betrayed him. Bowel cancer. Or as he told me, "Cancer will always get you in the end."

Wooly Bears, Not Birds

A clear, blue sky. The landscape softened by leaves and grasses turning from green to yellow and brown. The pleasant rustle of downed leaves underfoot. A perfect fall day to head to Oak Hammock Marsh in the Interlake just north of Winnipeg.

At this time of the year, The Marsh proves why it's an IBA (Important Bird Area). Hundreds of shore birds, thousands of ducks, and tens of thousands of geese stop here in southward migration every day.

As I walked a path to get the sun behind me and get more than just a silhouette of some ducks, I almost stepped on a woolly bear (*Pyrrharctic isabella*). It caused an intense flashback.

Thirty years ago, I strapped my two young daughters into their car seats and took them to The Marsh to show them the wonders of a fall Manitoba waterfowl migration.

The sky then was dark with geese, and their plaintive honking could be heard almost a kilometre away. I instructed my girls on the differences between the varieties of ducks and geese. I pointed out how some geese wiffle down onto the water. I showed them the dabbling ducks and the diving grebes, and I asked them to count the seconds the grebes were underwater. The girls couldn't have been less interested.

What caught their attention were the woolly bears. While I was gazing up, the girls were staring down at the little black and copper caterpillars (also known as woolly worms, fuzzy bears, and hedgehog caterpillars). They nodded as I preached, but I could see that they were fascinated by the soft feel of the woolly bears, by their funny, rolling way of walking, and the way they curled up into little balls when they were picked up. They liked the tickle of little feet as the caterpillars walked across the palms of their hands.

I didn't know much about caterpillars then, but I decided to make it a teaching moment anyway—even though what I told them was dead wrong.

The woolly bears, I said, were larvae that would turn into wondrous butterflies in the spring. (In fact, they become orangey-yellow tiger moths.) And I indicated that you could tell from their colours whether the winter would be warm or cold; the blacker they are, the longer and colder the winter will be. (In fact, the colouration of the thirteen segments of the woolly bears is the result of their age and feeding habits.)

For the rest of our time there I looked at birds to see if I could find a Ross's or a White-fronted Goose among all the Canadas or any lingering shorebirds (or beachies as some Brits call them). Meanwhile, my daughters searched for more caterpillars.

I didn't realize until we got home that they were not just searching, they were collecting. They were hoping to hide the woolly bears so that in spring their bedrooms would be full of "flutterflies." They were not just collectors, they were dreamers.

Sadly, their seatbelts had mashed most of the larvae (at least a dozen each) in their jacket pockets. Not many woolly bears survived the ride home and icky, greenish goo stained their jackets.

We only saved a few, putting them outside in the grass and hoping that their natural cryoprotectant (anti-freeze) would help them survive until spring.

By the next spring my daughters had forgotten their precious woolly bears.

Thirty years later they've forgotten the entire incident. I hope this chapter reminds them of the innocent and sometimes messy dreams of youth.

For my two daughters way back then, hope was a roomful of things with wings—beautiful, fragile butterfly wings. For me, along with poet Emily Dickinson, "Hope is the thing with feathers." Since I first read that poem, I've always had a special connection to it. That connection became even stronger when I moved to Winnipeg. As the poem goes on to say, "I've heard it in the chilliest land," and Winnipeg is the "chilliest" place I've ever lived.

I suppose I'm more of a literalist than the metaphorical Emily Dickinson. I read that first line of the poem backwards rather than forwards. The thing with feathers for me represents hope. Birds have kept me active and warm in Winnipeg. They've kept me from declining into pessimism and doubt. When I need a boost, there are always the birds.

I hope the essays in this book have conveyed some of the sense of possibility and wonder, some of the camaraderie and comfort that birds have provided. Through birding, I've had some great adventures, met some wonderful people, seen some memorable places, animals, and birds. A life touched by birds is a better life.

Acknowledgements

The following essays have appeared in slightly different forms and with different titles in the following publications:

"My Birding Bruises." Reprinted with permission of *Birdwatching Digest*.

"The Passenger Pigeon Apocalypse." Revised from *The Birds of Manitoba* and reprinted with permission of Manitoba Avian Research Committee and Nature Manitoba.

"House Sparrows: Basic, Economy-sized Birds," "Black-capped Chickadees: Cheerful, Little Fluffballs," "Mallards and Other Tippy Ducks," "Nuthatches and Woodpeckers: Birds with Sticky Feet," "A Great Blue Heron Returns Before Ice-out," "American White Pelicans: Ghost Riders in the Sky," "Eyeball to Eyeball with a Short-eared Owl," "Merlins and Other Bird Brains," "Corvids: The Smartest Birds in the World," "Kathy and the Pileated Woodpeckers," "Atlantic Puffins: Clowns of the Sea," "Mississippi Kites: Alien Visitors," "A Greylag and Other Wild Goose Chases," "Apapanes and Other Hawaiian Birds," "Fast and Furious Falcons," "A Fall-out of Spring Warblers," "Larks Larking," "Churchill, Manitoba: A Birder's Chilly Paradise," "The Big Spit: At a Birding Festival," "Looking for Pootoos: A Deadly Encounter," "Scary Surprise on an Amazonian Birding Tower," "Common Grackles: Unloved and Unwanted," "Wrynecks and Other Jinx Birds," "What's in a Name?," "Bird Feeder Freeloaders," "The Old Man and the Lek," "Old Jack and the Crow with One Leg," "Woolly Bears, Not Birds," Revised and Expanded from Green Mountain Digital Blogs. Printed with permission of National Audubon Society.

Special thanks to all those who helped make me a better birder and this a better book: Jamis, Sharon and Sarah at Turnstone Press, Charlie Rattigan, Dennis Cooley, Michelle and Leah Walz, John Weier, Rudolf Koes, Peter Taylor, Brad Carey, Andy Courcelles, Richard Staniforth, George Holland, Robert Taylor, Bob Nero, Christian Artuso, Ward Christianson, Marlene Waldron, Rob Parsons, Bob Talbot, and Liz Morash.